UNKNOWN TRANSACTIONS

UNKNOWN TRANSACTIONS

Avoiding Scams Through Understanding

KELECHI ONONUJU

authorHOUSE®

AuthorHouse™ LLC
1663 Liberty Drive
Bloomington, IN 47403
www.authorhouse.com
Phone: 1-800-839-8640

Published by AuthorHouse 07/08/2013

ISBN: 978-1-4817-6771-2 (sc)
ISBN: 978-1-4817-6772-9 (e)

Library of Congress Control Number: 2013911264

DEDICATION

For *Chidochiri*, *Munachimso* and *Nnamdi*

Contents

PART 3
FEATURES OF SCAM BUSINESSES

PART 4
SCAM BUSINESS AS A CRIME.

PART 5
AVOIDING SCAMS

THE FACTS

- 'A good lie is based in truth'
- Scams are on the increase and the scammers are getting more sophisticated.
- Scam schemes are now being set-up like genuine businesses worldwide.
- A single scam can take on different forms, so there is no way to define the shape or form the offer or presentation will take.
- The modern business person must still do business globally irrespective of scams rampancy.
- Many individuals are presently in ongoing scams without their knowledge.
- Certain features are common in scam business transactions.
- The confident way to avoid scams is by understanding scam business processes

Avoid scam handbook.
A must read for the business person.
Read this before that next business venture.
Understanding scam business processes.

PREFACE

A *scam* is a clever and dishonest plan for making money (a fraudulent business looking scheme solely designed for extorting another participant in the business). A scam is designed to trick you into giving away your money or your private details. Scams succeed because they look real and appeal to your needs and desires. The people who run these scam schemes are very manipulative; knowing the right buttons to push to produce the response they want. They are also masters in faking personalities, identities and documents.

A *scammer* is a person who perpetrates a scam. A scammer is a swindler, a trickster, a con artist, a confidence man, a con man and a deceiver. A *scam target* is someone the scammer aims to deceive; a person the scammer hopes to lure into a scam by sending a proposal. A *scam victim* will be regarded as one who has already lost money in a scam business, has made payments to the scammer or has made payments following the scammer's directives. A person who is still a target, already involved in the business process, dealing with the scammer, but has not yet made payments to the scammer will be regarded as a *prospective scam victim*.

Fraud is common in scams and can be defined as intentional misrepresentation for the purpose of gain or the crime of obtaining money or some other benefit by deliberate deception. The introduction of Internet, electronic commerce (ecommerce) and electronic business (ebusiness) has expanded the rampancy of frauds.

There are detailed news, publications, videos, documentaries and descriptions of various scams. So many literatures have explained how best avoiding scams, but people still get scammed daily. We cannot ignore the fact that scams take on various forms; a particular scam can be presented or introduced in several ways to a scam target. It has also become noticeable that most people let their guard down against scams easily when they start waiting for a particular presentation of a scam.

Scammers and con artists are like people you see and interact with everyday. It is therefore important to understand certain observations, processes, patterns, and some features common to scam businesses.

An in depth understanding of the how and why the scam victims fell for the scams and the grand design of the scammers or conmen is the best education in avoiding scams.

The majority of the processes scammers adopt are derived from genuine business processes. The world is a global village; the modern business persons must do business locally as well as internationally. They must now use different mechanisms to carry out their operations; meeting their business partners physically or not, but ensuring that mutually beneficial relationships ensue. This is one problem the global business has had to face.

Theft is getting obsolete; the new trend adopted by thieves is to induce their would-be victims into giving them what they would have stolen from them. The scammers' primary objective is for you to release your money or property into their hands. To make their unsuspecting victims do this, the scammers will adopt many strategies, pretences to lure their scam targets, prospective victims or victims to comply accordingly. In most cases these strategies resemble genuine business processes.

Globalization has made it so that the modern business person cannot only do business locally but worldwide. New businesses with totally new business transactions are emerging every day. It is obvious that the modern business persons must carry on with their operations, regardless of the rampancy of scams. Likewise, it is clear that many factors in our new global village will remain unknown, since no one can accurately estimate the intentions and authenticity of another—a person you have not seen or met before. For instance, one cannot refuse to use the modern ways of transferring money in the modern globalized world because of scams. No, you must still use credit cards, debit cards and the other modern means of transferring money to do your business. Yet you need to take notice and be aware of anything that may sound suspicious.

It is now mandatory for anyone involved in a business transaction to have a means of knowing what they are doing, or at least, have a good knowledge of the intentions of his or her new business partner. The modern business person must try to deduce this unknown partner's intentions from the ongoing business processes and procedures.

In this book, different scams, observations, patterns and features, common in scam businesses are discussed. Also, this book will offer the reader a better understanding of scams and how to avoid them. Scams are best avoided when one understands clearly the scammers' intentions from the ongoing business processes.

ACKNOWLEDGEMENT

Unknown Transactions: *avoiding scams through understanding*, is a product of valuable detailed insights deduced from news, articles, court judgments, scam stories, stories told, reported experiences, research and careful investigations.

I acknowledge all those who have contributed the material, articles, announcements and publications which dealt with the scam problems and their avoidance. Good works I must confess!

To God Almighty I am grateful as this book was a vision that had so many hitches. An opportunity to give this insight into scam problems and possible solutions that will enable the reader, understand new realities and avoid financial losses which is presently hindering economic growths worldwide.

I also thank all those who told me stories about their past experiences in scam businesses in one way or the other, knowingly and unknowingly. This includes scam targets, prospective scam victims, scam victims, policemen, workers, politicians, business persons and scammers. I really appreciate your stories and their contents. As you all read this book, you will understand better, the need that we share such stories. I will also thank those behind the magnificent results the research provided.

NOTE TO READERS

This book is based on my own observations. Since the deductions and analyses I have made are strictly personal, I cannot say they are a hundred percent correct. These analyses stem from years of observations of both genuine business and scam business transactions, from books and reports I have read, been told or heard. Throughout my analyses, I have noticed a common pattern evolving in these reported scams which gave me the idea and the basis for writing this book.

I am not an expert in criminology, psychology, sociology, law enforcement or finance. I am not a guru of any form. I have been scammed several times myself. As a victim, an observer, an investigator, a reader and a businessman, I have come to the conclusion that some features were common in scan businesses when compared to genuine businesses.

Business transaction methods evolve everyday and there is no particular method acceptable worldwide. I can only say that there are methods perceived as acceptable generally, and they should be thoroughly checked before entering into any business transactions to avoid scams.

Instances, examples and illustrations used in this book are all fictitious. Names used and places mentioned are also fictitious and do in no way relate to anyone anywhere whatsoever. Scam stories in this book are short, as I try to hit the main points in explaining the necessary points and allow the reader the advantage of relating to the same story in other situations.

The majority of the discussions in this book are not only unknown to the many scam victims but also unknown to many scammers who might never understand why one victim willingly released what others in same situation refused to release. Only thorough analyses of successful scam stories can you gain awareness and avoid scams.

At the outset of any business, any participant in that business can be a prospective scam victim. It should be that prospective scam victim's decision not to make the scam victims' list. This book will assist anyone in not becoming that next scam victim. As the world globalizes further, many business transactions will become more unknown transactions.

INTRODUCTION

Most scams are spontaneous they say;—*If spontaneity is too good to be left to chance, then, let us form a pattern of following spontaneity.* We need to obtain enough information about our other business partner, before, during and after the business transaction.

One of the greatest con artists put it this way:

'I only took money from those who could afford it and were willing to go in with me in schemes they fancied would fleece others. They wanted money for its own sake; I wanted it for the luxuries and pleasures it would afford me. They were seldom concerned with human nature. They knew little—and cared less—about their fellow man. If they had been students of human nature, if they had given more time to companionship with their fellows and less to the chase of the almighty dollar, they wouldn't have been such easy works' ('YELLOW KID' WEIL (1875-1976).

No one should underestimate the power and impact of his or her financial decisions. Your success or failure in life is affected by the few choices you make in your life. To succeed you must manage your finances well and to manage your finances well you must have the knack to differentiate scams from genuine business transactions.

In certain theology, there is **divine giving** and there is **demonic giving**. The ability to use your finances judiciously and positively for mankind's progress is a divine gift few persons have. Few have the ability to detect scams without much effort; such qualities are divine to such persons. Also, it is common for people you assisted not to be grateful because in reality, they had no problem that needed assistance when you helped them. They simply deceived you into a demonic giving while you thought you were assisting them.

It might appear that many successful rich persons have a percentage of inbuilt **scam detecting mechanism**. The personality and aura of a rich man plus his exotic environment demand a hundred percent, absolute courage from a scammer to pull a scam on the rich man. You just have to be like him or near him to pull such scams through. If you check, you will discover that a good percentage of business proposals presented directly to very rich men are genuine, never scams.

Let us attribute this to the fact that rich men do not read their mails themselves nor answer their calls directly, and to the effect their irresistible charm has on the interlocutor. I regard these and other qualities as their self-protection mechanisms, which, if not present will expose that rich person to scams. Likewise, I have observed the opposite to be true in people who do not want society to know they are rich. They hide their money due to its origin and in that process start entering shady deals which will finally expose them to several scams. Some corrupt world leaders make up a great majority of this group; they steal so much money while in government and end up being broke two or three years later after leaving government offices. At times, I wonder why, and it all boils down to being victims of scams from all corners and to their inability to radiate that rich man's charm due to their funds' origin. I do not even exempt the foreign banks and governments where they deposited these stolen funds in scamming most of the money out of them, too. It is like being wide open for a sucker punch from anyone. My personal opinion is that if you have money, let the society know and use it as it should be used. I refuse to accept that very rich people are in danger. I see the opposite; they are in very safe hands as the world realizes their importance. This is by the way and moreover, my personal opinion.

We often attribute so much to luck; scam detecting mechanism can be unconsciously implanted in a business person over several years of successful business practice. Others must learn the symptoms of scan businesses and practice to being able to detect scams as they appear and reappear in daily business transactions nowadays.

No one is above scams as they come in different forms and shapes. Many successful scams are seen by their scam victims as business failures or transactions that failed to materialize, while some scams appear as direct scams the police authorities and courts get to entertain.

In explaining some features common in scam businesses, we will also try to relate or compare them with observations common to genuine business transactions. They are intertwined I will say and so many similarities appear in both. One needs to be thorough to detect which transaction you are into. It might require only some minor homework, or a one-on-one check which you can do mentally in seconds. Ask the right questions and await the answers that will indicate whether a scam is in progress. If it requires two or more questions, ask them, at least to ensure that you are not wasting your precious time in a scam business transaction. The loss might be very negligible to your finances but will impact greatly on the scammer's finances and confidence in further scams.

Some scams are criminal in nature while others are not. A scan can present itself as a normal genuine business transaction. The conditions can be so palatable that you will happily part with your money without complaints whatsoever. I have come to understand that many scams from the outset were carefully arranged to appear so and create such impressions. Many scam victims still believe that scams were businesses gone badly; they therefore, bear no grudges against the scammers, thinking they were and are still good business partners. Of course, genuine businesses go bad, too, but it is not always true that a genuine business gone bad requires monetary input. You can start to smell scam.

Scams generally come out as one or a mixed combination of these simple terminologies: obtaining by trust or by tricks; betrayal of confidence; manufactured expenses; different from appearance; high yield investments; income earners; money transfer; occult manipulations; self imposed bills; wise investors; profit making original; come-and-buy; manufactured scarcity; high price offer; big business deal, and so on. Most people that were scammed were introduced to the scam business via a communication medium. We will discuss some of these mediums which include mails, emails, mobile phone calls, SMS, physical contact and even genuine business manifests.

Financial independence is an ultimate goal for every reasonable person, it will help you and your loved ones escape those financial difficulties that are common and exists for most people. Financial independence will also allow you to enjoy yourself and live your desired lifestyle. The final financial success everyone wants is a journey and never a destination. It is a hard journey that has so many obstacles stretching even to the final destination.

It is necessary for everyone to understand that scams and scam proposals are becoming daily affairs everywhere. Many people will find it difficult to understand that scams are everywhere because of differences in what each of us regards as scam. There have been cases where very wealthy persons saw paying government taxes as being scammed. Their feeling might be that if others had worked as hard as them, they too would have been rich and maybe there would not have been need for taxation and the provision of social welfare services to the less privileged.

This simple reason has made so many wealthy persons leave their countries of origin to live in tax havens.

Distribution of wealth is never even and this inequality is what without delegation, many, including nature, assign to themselves to level off. Robin Hood, according to history, might have tried to redistribute wealth in old Britain. Some do this the wrong way, while I believe others try to redress these inequalities the right way. The revolution of wealth remains a constant. New millionaires are being made daily while many old millionaires are losing status.

Scams and scammers have always existed in time. They are not new things to the world; they are old things being presented in modified ways. ***Scams have always been around and will continue to be around for a very long time to come.*** They will not go away; one just has to know exactly what they are and be well equipped to avoid them in all business dealings and transactions. This is the best anyone can hope for. The continuous presence of scams has created the need to device a sort of self assessing mechanism to keep yourself, your finances, your transactions and ventures, safe from scammers and deceivers alike.

Initially, it was believed money transfer scams occur only in Nigeria. It has now become clearer to other nations and world authorities, that with scam business networking, even their nationals are involved. Similar scams have now been observed in most large cities of the world where advanced law enforcement agencies are vigorously pursuing and capturing these sometimes very elusive culprits. Scam proposals are now originating from almost all countries. It is as if everyone and even governments are involved. As a matter of fact, not everyone is involved and governments are not involved. The truth is that very few people are involved but the internet has modified and simplified scams. A huge scam can now be set up in minutes using the internet facilities. A bank account can be opened in minutes using the internet. Millions of emails can now be sent at once by clicking a 'send' button. Exact samples of most delicate documents are on the internet if you know how to search for and reproduce them. The new world order is that of awareness and availability.

Scam is bourgeois, it is complex, it is complicated and very much undefined as it appears in many court judgments—*'the victim should have known from the outset that the business was too bourgeois to be real'*. The difficult question now is, how one judges a business that is bourgeois? So many genuine businesses with little capital investment have generated huge profits, running into several thousands and millions. Many people have purposely avoided businesses that run into millions in order to avoid being scammed, but scamming does not depend or focus on any particular amount. Scam can thrive in any transaction irrespective of the business worth. The amount mentioned in a scam proposal solely depends on the scammer's design as he or she tries to make the scam proposal appetizing to the scam target.

The number of scam victims keep increasing daily remains a problem. Avoiding scams by mere lookouts for particular scam presentations might fail at times because a particular scam can be presented in different ways. The same scam can be presented to an unsuspecting scam target in over a hundred ways. It therefore makes no sense to be on the lookout for a particular scam proposal presentation as most films, radio, TV programs and books try to inform the public. In as much as these programs are very helpful, but an understanding of the entire scam business processes is a better guide in preventing being scammed. It will enable you to carry on with your business on a more secure footing while enabling to identify the alluring scams lurking around the corner.

Understanding scam business processes will assist you in doing business with any unknown business partner. Scams as a matter of fact, are not perpetrated by particular methods, mediums or even societal class.

Thorough analyses of successful scams will show that each and every scam was unique to the scammed victim and the scammer. Each scam victim-scammer relationship is unique and cannot be easily imitated in another scam business. No two successful scams were exactly the same in process, psychology and execution.

Human beings vary and there is no way, anyone can replicate or expect a replica of a past scam situation. Also, people have different reasons for entering into the same business. These inabilities create room for the complexity in understanding scam businesses. Still, there are common features of scam businesses that are undisputed. For instance, it is possible these days to ship ten containers of raw material cocoa to your importing business partner in China without seeing or meeting him for a second and still get paid successfully. You can also ship just one container of raw material cocoa to another business partner in the same China and never hear from him again. Was there a difference in these two importers from the same country? Yes, there were differences in their importation business processes, of course, that only a trained observer's eyes could have seen.

Scam victims suffer diminished mental and moral capacities. The majority of the victims graduate to desperation as this masterful game of deceit wears them down, devastating them. Traumatic disorder is a common feature of scam victims, resulting from constant barrage of insomnia, anxiety, fear, panic and premeditated manipulations. A traumatized and destroyed scam victim's situation can be avoided if you really understand what the scammer planned. I also think the scammers are sick; I have come across scammers who get very desperate once their prospective victims are not responding adequately. The scammer also has anxieties. As the scam victim or prospective scam victim enters the realms of imagination regarding the ***promised gain***, the scammer navigates through the realms of ***expected extortions*** from the victim. In most cases, their relationship lack conscious feeling since they may have never met each other physically. It is common that both parties cannot evaluate or estimate the damage they are causing each other.

Never forget that the scammer in any scam business has privileged information because he or she is the only participant in the business aware of the scam nature of the business. There are also greedy victims who entered say money transfer scam businesses 'knowingly', with wonderful ideas that the world would never have known, had it been the money transfer business was real and not fictitious. Maybe they would have killed their business partners for the transferred money or kept the loot for themselves. As I mentioned earlier, the inner thoughts of the scam victims and the scammers are vast, complex and complicated, for every human is unique. In later chapters we will try to deduce what thoughts might have crossed these minds as the business (scam) ensued.

The author, Brian Wizard in his book 'Don't Be Scammed, Be informed' carefully narrated the similarity between a 419-scam victim, an obsessive gambler and a drug user. While the latter two can be rehabilitated through retraining, community and family support, the former is cured by getting rid of the brainwashing implanted in him or her by the scammer.

Furthermore, a scam victim and a gambler are both chasing their past expenses and in the process incurring more expenses to chase again. A scam victim's chase is defined as a promised gain—and because of past expenses in the chase, the scam victim will term 'business expenses' the chase will continue. On the other hand, a gambler is not expecting any promised gain; just chasing past losses and hoping for a better fortune that is not defined. Chronic gamblers only want to win back their past losses and if possible make some profit. The scam victims and gamblers differ from drug users, who are busy chasing that same first-intake feeling the drug had on them the very first time they ingested it. All are worthless chases. The drug user will find it difficult to re-achieve that first-intake feeling by using more drugs. This is why it is easy for a rehabilitated drug user to return to old habits because the same first-intake feeling can come back after a long period of abstinence in rehabilitation. The scam victim chase is worthless because there has never been any business in the first place, so business expenses are not applicable here and no promised gain is coming. The gambler also will only incur more losses as he or she chases previous losses. The gambler, ultimately, will lose value for money; this will make a previous loss of $10,000 to be now worth $50,000 in the gambler's eyes. This gambler will never take a $15,000 win home because in the gambler's eyes, the real loss is $50,000 and not $10,000. The chronic gambler never forgets to monetize all commitments in chasing his or her past losses. Quit is the name of the game for the scam victim, the gambler and the drug user. Casinos and gambling houses are like entering into scam businesses. Only internal fraud can wreck a casino and never gamblers' winnings. Likewise, only the knowledge that the business is a scam can rescue a scam victim.

These locally and internationally acclaimed scam schemes are now being operated worldwide. Africans, Americans, Asians, Australians, Caribbean's, Europeans, etc., are all involved: Why? It makes profit and everyone likes profit. Huge profits, as a matter of fact, because in most scam businesses, the scammer's investments are very small compared to the profit to be made, should a victim fall for the scam. Same cost-profit ratio is directly proportionate to the investments in most scams. Whenever the scammer invests heavily in a scam scheme, the expected gain from the scam victim(s) is also very high.

In *Part 1* of this book, we look at certain gaming mechanisms scams have incorporate or rather certain misconceptions, basics, so many people have completely misunderstood that has encouraged the thriving of scam businesses. *Part 2* is how one gets into scam businesses, the introduction mediums, different types of scams, scamming processes, extortions, victims' naivety, types of scam payments, the scammers manipulations, and the meaning of actions. Part 2 also gives detailed insight on commitments and their roles in making scams successful. In *Part 3*, we look at some common features of scam businesses everyone should look out for. Many persons come across these features in their business transactions but they are unable to decipher the meaning of the information. Part 3 will help to decipher these business process features in old and present business dealings to know if they were, or are scams or not. We will also look at the adamant progressive in Part 3 who refuses to leave an unproductive business venture alone, upon all the signals, symptoms and warnings to desist from such business by loved ones and the authorities.

Finally, we look at scams as serious crimes they ought to be in **Part 4**. Why scams are serious and not serious for some authorities. Why some scammers go free. Why many call scams 'white collar crimes'. Why the blind justice cannot clamp down on scam businesses and eradicate these menaces. We also look at why some scams are conveniently prosecuted while others are not. **Part 5** will deal with some dangerous myths and assumptions people have that lead them into scams. We also look at what these assumptions should be in the bid to avoid scams.

Scams are full of *unknown transactions*; where you cannot accurately ascertain the intentions of your unknown business partner nor can you completely verify all that is said, agreed and promised. Unknown transactions, as business might work out well, they might also not work out, and they can also be scams from origin. As the world globalizes further, more businesses will get unknown and transactions in such unknown businesses more unknown. Therefore the need to understand the scam business processes; the commitments, victims' naivety, scammers' ideology, emotional involvements, the participants' preliminary psychology, the advantages and disadvantages of actions, are very important.

A strong awareness, understanding, and prevention of the schemes, offers, methods, processes developed by a person, persons, group and companies to use to extort or take money you have worked so hard for, is the beginning of **real financial freedom.**

PART 1

A GAMING MECHANISM

It is a fact that so many persons, a good majority of us have totally misunderstood certain underlining principles that should naturally guide our actions and attitude towards finance. Scams thrive on the concept of 'rich equals success, unless we redress our attitude towards money.

'If a person gets his attitude towards money straight, it will help straighten out almost every other area in his life' (BILLY GRAHAM)

In this part, we look at these mechanisms that have encouraged these short comings and provided grounds for dishonesty and deceit as seen in scams.

CHAPTER 1

WEALTH AND MONEY

Wealth is defined as a large amount of money and or property that a person or an entity owns. It is the state of being rich. It is having a lot of money and possessions.

A wealthy person is a successful person by world standards. Whether through business, inheritance, charity, gift, etc., as long as you are rich, the world sees you as successful. The life of a rich person equals comfort. Almost everything is within reach. This is what matters to most of us and drives the majority of us. The ability to pay for goods and services is a priority to most people, educated or not, literate or not, exposed or not and developed or not.

Human beings are also driven by the desire to have the ability to possess not just enough but more than enough goods and services at their disposal. This desire to possess *more than enough* goods and services we will refer to as *Enzyme G*.

It is the quantity of this enzyme in a person that the scammers search for when picking their victims. If need be, the scammer will make an individual search but in most cases, the scammer will employ mass search or random sampling, based on self-content selection. The individuals with the desired quantity of Enzyme G will select themselves by responding to the scammer's proposals. Enzyme G is present in all men and women but more active in some people than in others. Rich people, comfortable people and even poor people can have high Enzyme G levels. Enzyme G is the major factor that drives people toward possessing wealth. Societal and environmental influences also play major roles in the development of Enzyme G in anyone. If you live in a society where all they talk about is the rich and how they are rewarded, irrespective of their wealth source, then the development of your Enzyme G might be distorted. The reverse is true when the environment is not conducive to the development of your Enzyme G. Enzyme G is also greedy and gullible.

In over 70% of successful scam cases, you will notice that the scam victims just wanted more money or to be precise, they wanted ***more easy money***. Maybe, they had too much Enzyme G or the story they were told in the scam proposal for more money seemed easier than the usual way of earning their money. We can say these scam victims were not poor persons but persons with good income. Unfortunately, people who are scammed are mostly people with good stable incomes.

Many people have been raised in law-abiding societies, and they have made serious efforts to teach their children to be law-abiding citizens, but as the world globalizes, there are certain things that can only be learnt on the streets.

A native African adage says; ***'At times it is good that bad things happen so that kids will know what exactly bad things are'***. The easiest way for a child to learn that stealing is a bad thing is for that child to witness where a thief is being held. A little fire burn is the best lesson a child can learn in avoiding fire. There are still those few people who learn from the experience of others. They are exceptional and naturally gifted persons. It is not easy and a great gift anyone can have.

No matter how anyone sees it, the fact remains that ***wealth is made when income greatly exceeds expenses***. Income and expense are directly proportional, making it difficult to achieve wealth unless an income haven can be achieved at minimal cost or expense. It is this income haven everyone is looking for and which the scammer tries to provide. We should also understand that locating an income haven is not easy in an enlightened world. People do not allow you to proceed toward an income haven when they are well aware of the benefits associated with that haven. If they are your workers, be ready for salary increases as they will try everything possible to narrow the difference between income and expenses as long as they are aware of the benefits you get from their work. It is based on this that anyone looking for income havens to create wealth, must maneuver a way that will allow their income to exceed expenses in those havens.

Many countries achieved income havens by colonialism. Other nations and individuals attain income havens using technology, know-how, oppression, suppression, military occupation, population, confidentiality, misinformation, and so on. The main objective was to ensure that income greatly exceeded expenses in whatever they were doing.

Literally, for you to make money, someone somewhere gave up some money. If your bank account reads (+) $5 million then somewhere else, somebody or several bank accounts put together must read (-) $5 million total. The end scenario now depends on whether there was satisfaction for those who parted with $5 million. If they are satisfied, no problems, but if they are not satisfied, then problems will emerge. They might have been scammed or duped into parting with their $5 million because they did not receive satisfaction after the expenditure.

Most people are guilty of misunderstanding wealth and what it should be. Parents have taught kids how to succeed in life but failed to teach them about money and its purpose. Parents have also failed to teach their kids 'the streets' where everything happens and where Enzyme G plays a major role. Wealth gets lost and made every day. Parents have made their fortune over a number of years, which their children will lose in a matter of months at the hands of advanced scammers because they lack a financially healthy mind and are not 'streetwise'. Being **streetwise** is having the knowledge that unbelievable things are possible elsewhere; that documents can be forged, that their best friend can be a scammer. Many people have no inkling or shield against any of these eventualities and they often think business ventures are just good willed and automatic such as they were taught in school. The world is changing fast; everyone must be aware that people will do business globally and not only in their 'straight' environment. These days one must now do business with people they do not know, have never met and these business transactions are expected to be successful.

In many societies, wealth is classified into two categories; genuine and ill gotten. However, societies should not fail to explain what is genuine and what is ill gotten. How can people believe the government when that same government honors and celebrates ill gotten wealth? This is why many are involved in scams and many still fall for scams without knowing. Maybe governments should declare openly the percentage of profit expected from any genuine business transaction. Maybe people should be made to understand that any business in which you have invested a few thousands to reap millions as profit is illegal. Maybe profit-making should be regulated to prevent scams.

Do genuine businesses with extremely high profit margins exist? This is another question to which only selected few know the right answer. The selected few who know the answer keep quiet, allowing the scammers to provide answers to the people seeking an answer to this question. Many have made money through bad means, later legitimizing the money and ending up being great personalities. Sports men and women who used enhancement drugs to become champions are even proud to admit they did so, they are even earning more from selling their biographies and granting interviews where they explain how they cheated.

Wealth making businesses and scams thrive along two parallel lines; you just have to be on the right line to guarantee wealth. Many people easily jump from one line to the other. Apart from fresh creation of wealth, which is available these days, for wealth to be created somewhere there must be wealth foregone elsewhere. Loss simply depends on what the affected victim calls satisfaction. As one can comfortably pay $200 for a chair, so can another pay $2000 for the same chair and both will still be satisfied proud owners of similar chairs.

Many huge business establishments, in many countries, have acquired their wealth through ill gotten gains from poorer, developing countries elsewhere through scams of which these countries were ignorant. For instance, many African rebel leaders impoverished their people by losing fortunes to fictitious arms dealers who never delivered any arms. Instead, these scammers set them up and their rebellions never succeeded. Some of those fictitious arms dealers used such fortunes to establish huge, successful businesses in their respective countries of origin; these businesses are still very much operational today. A man who steals from government coffers and establishes a successful business, employing about 10,000 workers, will always be regarded as an important man in that society. Often, the legitimate government will have no other option than to incorporate him as an important personality—at least for having created so many jobs. Moreover, employees of the man's business establishment will only harm you if you try to tamper with that business. "Government of the people for the people", remember?

Ill-gotten gain does not scare most people anymore because legitimizing such profits has become easier. Please do not lose your money carelessly to scammers, thinking that the scammers will be seen or are seen as persons with ill-gotten wealth. The respect a scammer gets in the world today depends on the scammer's usage of the extorted money. Also, do not overlook or underestimate some highly regarded personalities; thinking they could not possibly scam you. They are major scams or large scale scams perpetrated by the very rich. Moreover, it is easier for them to scam you, put the scam money to judicious use and even receive recognition from their governments.

In trying to become wealthy, ensure you have a financially healthy mind, decide on the type of wealth-making venture you want, check everyone thoroughly and never assume some people cannot scam you. Do not exhibit overgrown Enzyme G. Scammers can easily detect an overgrown Enzyme G and set a ***scam stage*** in minutes to scam you. Enzyme G can equally grow to scamming levels overnight without anyone's knowledge.

Rich people do scams also. Many very rich men have been imprisoned for fraudulent activities. You might wonder how this is possible, and any other reason will be given but the fact is that the rich man became a fraudster because he wanted more easy money—simple. It is also possible he might have lost his previous wealth and remained in hiding while everyone thought he was still the rich man he once was. These are common occurrences. What exactly should we term the siphoning processes many corrupt leaders use in embezzling their country's resources? Is it that they are not rich or they possess a large amount of Enzyme G?

Only one thing is common in the excessive chase for wealth, and that is greed. The ever growing desires to have more than enough goods and services.

Wealth is relative, so I see no reason for the competition to be richer than your peer. In as much as you have $2 million does not mean that another person with $2,000 is not happy. Problems vary according to your status. Many farmers do not have cash but they have food crops that can last them for months and they are happy. Equally, there are multi-millionaires who desperately chase more wealth as if they were penniless. One does not need millions to live comfortably. A thorough study will show that most of the very rich people never planned being very rich from the beginning. The majority only planned to make a good living out of whatever they were doing, which later developed into a multi-million dollar venture.

The first question everyone should ask is 'how much money do I really need to live a good life?' You must ask yourself this question and you must provide an answer to it, unless you have a financially unhealthy mind. It is very important that everyone affix a definite amount as the amount of money he or she will need to live comfortably for the rest of his or her life. This target amount will act as a guide, giving you a financially healthy mind, because every money-making proposal is not business to a financially healthy mind.

A man went to a priest for his confessions; he confessed that he had sinned. The confessant claimed to be in custody of a certain box of money belonging to his former boss who died in a car accident. The confessant said he was the car driver and the only survivor of the car accident where his boss died. Crying, he said that since then he has not had the courage to return this box to the family of his deceased boss. The priest asked him where the box was presently and he said it was in police custody, but he knew a police officer who could assist him in bringing out the box for $1,000. According to the confessant, the real content of the box was unknown to the police. The priest gave him the $1,000 and told him to bring the box so that they would do the 'right thing'. The confessant brought the box later on to the priest. When they opened the box, the content was wads of black paper, the size of US dollar bills, and directives on how to clean it. In short, the confessant now claimed to remember how his late master did it, and that he knew where his late master bought the chemicals he normally uses to clean such black papers in the past. Convinced, the priest started sponsoring the cleaning of the black papers and in the process lost close to $116,000 to the confessant who was a scammer from day one.

This priest for all his good nature had a very serious financially unhealthy mind. This is a big problem and will always hurt such people. The priest totally missed the meaning of being a priest. He could have simply directed the confessant to send the box to the deceased family and report back to him. Was the priest chasing wealth or trying to experiment?

A seventy five year old man caught stealing a very huge sum of money is sick. He should be treated in a hospital. Prison is not the answer here, but a proper psychological assessment and treatment is. This is money the old man does not need if he had a financially healthy mind.

In the said business, Mr. Sterner and his Nigerian business partners finally agreed—upon Mr. Sterner's insistence—that Mr.

Sterner should retain 25% of the transferred sum for his assistance. Mr. Sterner now looked forward to celebrating his seventy fifth birthday in a grand style. In that business with these Nigerian partners, Mr. Sterner lost $1,800,000 to his Nigerian business partners who were actually scammers from day one.

Mr. Sterner had a financially unhealthy mind. He did not really understand the meaning of wealth and its purpose. Getting 25% in a business with *criminal undertone* at that age is a total misconception of money making.

There are businesses the self righteous man should not be involved, there are businesses in which a doctor should not be involved, and there are businesses in which a lawyer should not be involved, etc. The problem here is that when you start doing a business in which one in your status should not be involved, then you have opened yourself 'very wide' for the sucker punch coming soon. While doing contracts, *there is nothing as good as a doctor (medical director) quietly telling a contractor that he or she cannot for any private gains, inflate the costs of those medical equipments because lives might be lost if there is delay in delivering medical care.*

Wealth, what it is, what it is used for and how much of it one needs at anytime are grossly misunderstood by many of us, creating room for scams and scammers. Understanding these rules will enable you to have a financially healthy mind. You will not see all profit money-making ventures as worthwhile and you will not be that easy to scam.

CHAPTER 2

SEEKING FINANCIAL FREEDOM

'Falling for a ruse often takes intelligence and imagination'—a sense of the possible reward.

Financial freedom seekers easily see opportunities they think are solutions.

The majority of people is seeking financial freedom and in their quest will accept the humiliation of being conned or scammed with a sense of resignation. They learn the bitter lesson that there is no such thing as a free lunch and that they were scammed by their own greed in making fast money. The best way to deceive anyone is to play upon his or her insecurity because most people have insecurities. Financial insecurity is common for many.

In the bid of seeking financial freedom you need to set a definite target—the amount of money that will enable you to solve all your needs in life wisely. It can be millions or any amount you desire but set this target as a guide for your financial ventures. It takes real planning, and honesty to know all your present and future needs to set this target amount. Do this and let it guide you. Do not jump into any business that comes your way to avoid being scammed. We have discussed this in the last chapter, so it is not new, but a reminder.

Financial ignorance is very common for most financial freedom seekers. How many university graduates have been tutored in the required skills to achieve financial success? Very few! Many credit card holders do not know how the credit and interests work. Making an 'A' grade in college finance is quite different from financial awareness. How many financial freedom seekers are aware of known investments with slow but steady returns? The majority of financial freedom seekers have little or no knowledge about investments, treasury bills, bonds, insurances, government monetary regulations and policies, acceptable payment systems—locally and internationally—money orders, money transfer regulations, money laundering laws, anti-fraud laws, etc. Anyone seeking financial freedom must be well informed or he or she might be gallivanting in ignorance. From some scam stories, I wonder how very educated people can believe that another legitimate government, elsewhere in the world, will pay them $85 million 'cash'. Even the legitimate owners of US Dollar bills cannot pay you that amount in cash.

It is in seeking financial freedom that most ill-informed people fall prey to businesses that are scams. They venture into investments without the right knowledge. It is clear that no investment is 100% guaranteed, the scammer knows it and gets creative accordingly. Certain ventures that worked in the past do not mean they will work in the present. A scammer will hit the jackpot if his or her scam proposal is the exact one the scam target or prospective scam victim prays to come across in achieving financial freedom.

In anyone's quest to seek financial freedom, be thorough, check the investment details thoroughly, visit firms and meet real people, check their references and certificates, or rather do your little homework on their authenticity. You will be surprised how useful these amateur investigations will be in your assessment.

Over 80% of internet users believe 100% of whatever they see on the internet. Some internet users believe the computer has processed and brought out the right answers. They seem to forget that the resulting information was previously fed in by someone else. What if the wrong information or distorted information was fed into the computer? They never consider that. So many people enter scam businesses without knowing, simply because they read somewhere on the internet that other people entered into the same venture and succeeded.

How many financial freedom seekers are aware that the internet concludes businesses these days? You can open a bank account on the internet, fund it, and withdraw, without physically stepping into any bank. The government tries to intervene and protect these cyberspace investors, but the scammers know their major advantage is greed and seeking financial freedom on the part of their preys.

Most businesses and proposals with very high returns on investments that will guarantee financial freedom must be scrutinized before venturing into them, as many are scams. There are recognized experts you can consult in your quest for financial freedom, they have offices and are ready to assist. Do not shy away from the fee you will pay these consultants to give you a professional advice. It is worth every cent rather than being scammed. (See Chapter 8—*Understanding Gains and Losses*)

Remember the saying; *'If the business sounds too good to be true, then it cannot be true'*.

The Ponzi scheme was very popular in the early and mid 20ᵗʰ century in certain countries. Later on it died because governments in those countries ensured it did not thrive further. Do you know that the Ponzi scheme came into some developing African countries in the early 1990s? Do you know that same Ponzi scheme will be new in some countries in the future? A massive Ponzi scheme was uncovered in India this year (2013). A professional Ponzi scheme scammer simply keeps looking for his or her Ponzi scheme paradise (where people want financial freedom the easy way) and such paradises still exist, as a matter of fact.

In a town in Nigeria with low literate rate, a man opened a community bank. This bank gave a 40% interest on a three month term deposit. People began depositing their money and genuinely received their capital plus the 40% interest three months later. It became the toast of the town. Everyone wanted to put their money there and get 40% interest. There was no need for anyone to be working when such ventures existed. Everything was as expected. No one could beat it. The mega banks lost their depositors, since they withdrew their monies and deposited it in this new community bank paying 40% interest. In five months of operation the liquidity of this community bank was in billions of Naira. No complaints because people kept receiving their capital plus interests as at when due. The line of depositors at the community bank was record breaking. This was a Ponzi scheme in full operation.

The community bank was simply paying earlier depositors with money deposited by later investors. The con man (scammer) who launched the community bank knew his scheme would soon be over but he had these sure bets;

- Only the government authorities could stop him.
- All depositors would never want their deposits plus interests at the same time.
- The community bank would be very popular in the eyes of the people.
- He set aside 100 million Naira monthly for himself from all the deposits.

The community bank owner as a con man knew these advantages would set him free, if need be. Six months after commencement of the community bank, as pressure against the community bank's mysterious business built up, the owner started displaying imported exotic cars in the community bank premises, claiming he was investing depositors' monies in importation and making the 40% profit he was giving as interests quarterly; mere disguise. The depositors themselves spread the news like wild fire and business boomed. Finally the D-day came; the government, under pressure from the mega banks struck. The government sealed the community bank's premises. The operation was illegal. They had neither licenses nor bank business books. Till today, the government is still trying to convince depositors that the community bank owner was a fraud. To worsen matters and exonerate himself further, the community bank owner said that the reported amount recovered from his premises as claimed by the government authorities was a lie. He said that he had twenty times that amount in the premises when the authorities sealed it. Depositors still blame the government for making them lose their deposits with the community bank.

Actually, not all depositors in this community bank were illiterates; there were also some very educated lecturers from the local community university (known authorities in Banking & Finance) who also deposited in this community bank.—Physical presentation of scam is very disarming and makes scam victims out of very educated and enlightened persons.

Some proposals that promise legitimate financial freedom are indirect scams, such as the one described above. They will definitely be closed by the government, shifting the blame from the original scam perpetrators. This particular scammer made his money as soon as the Ponzi scheme went into operation, waiting for government to act, just in time to exonerate him. The above is an example of massive scam presented in a genuine business fashion. Today the community bank owner, who has won elective posts, still enjoys a good name—'an honest, straight forward and genuine business man whose business was ruined by wicked government officials'.

Meanwhile in the same community bank, some depositors with low Enzyme G level gained, because they invested once, took their 40% profit and left before the scam bust. This is rare, because in such situations, 80-90% of the depositors rarely take their capital plus profit and leave. They just keep re-investing both the capital and interest paid. This is a frequent occurrence in such Ponzi schemes.

In seeking financial freedom, considering the present economic recession, you must beware of businesses ventures promising very high returns. Use the bank interest rates as a rough guide for estimating what the expected returns in investments should be. Once the level of promised profit gets too high, please check it carefully, do your investigations thoroughly before venturing into such investments. Watch out for these two conditions—the investment will have something for you to gain and you will be lucky to know about it. I know many people believe in 'normal rate of returns' while others believe in 'God', no matter the venture, but God helps those who help themselves.

The way we seek financial freedom can create room for scammers. Some businesses can generate very high profits, I admit, but such businesses are not common. Even where such businesses exist, the profit is not distributed carelessly nor does the profit maker advertise his or her money-making secrets to invite unnecessary competition. There are very rich people on earth today; maybe they can teach us how to acquire their money-making skills on webinars.

Two factors that must be present in seeking financial freedom are patience and planning. Everyone understands the meaning of patience. Likewise, everyone needs to understand that huge profit-making businesses are rarely part of good financial freedom plans. It is common sense that some businesses or investments cannot be true. Most scam victims sense this at the beginning and somehow they still go ahead with the business, only for their initial fear to materialize.

I once asked a scam victim, 'why did you still invest when you had such suspicion'. He replied, 'The guy sounded very honest'. I asked further, 'If he sounded honest, what then was your initial suspicion? He responded 'something was just not right in the whole investment proposal, but I could not identify it'.

Your 'sixth sense' told you that this is not real but you still went ahead, only to regret not to have listened to your sixth sense. The scam victim above is a very educated person and what he could not identify was 'homework prompting'. His instinct was telling him to do his homework but the profit to be made in the investment and the urgent need to utilize a wonderful opportunity for financial freedom overshadowed everything.

Homework Prompting occurs when your instincts still insist something is not right in the business venture irrespective of the clarity and transparency of the business proposal. Homework prompting simply means that you should do a thorough homework on the business before venturing into it.

A good number of scam victims, as the said businesses progressed suspected the business venture to be a scam but somehow suppressed their instincts and carried on with the business, only to be ultimately scammed. If you analyze them and if scam victims are honest, you will discover this as what happened in most successful scam cases

In seeking financial freedom you must develop your instinct the right way. Your instinct should know in seconds if certain things are not possible financially, such as a legitimate government paying you $85 million in cash. It might sound strange but you must listen to your instincts. *Your first protection against anything is instinct. A well developed instinct is the first observer that should instruct anyone on the homework to be performed on anything. In seeking financial freedom, develop your instinct to Homework prompting level.* (See Chapter 29—*Transaction Vigilance.*)

The vision of a promised gain and greed in seeking financial freedom are always eager to engage in a new business venture, while the developed instinct insists it must be verified. You might even be pardoned if you never suspected it was a scam during the whole process before you got scammed.

Let us consider seeking financial freedom as a process and never an end reached when one has multimillions.

Genuine businesses with huge profit margins are not for everyone's eye to see or for everyone's ear to hear. Moreover, you do not get introduced to such businesses by someone you do not know. Big profit businesses are not for distribution. Luck does not come like that. If you insist that big money-making is based mainly on luck, please buy a lottery ticket. It costs less and does not cause heart breaks.

CHAPTER 3

OBSESSION WITH SUCCESS AND MONEY CHASING

Many people are obsessed with success and want to tell their own success stories, such as wealthy people do. But, most successful stories of wealth are true cases of hard work. Hard work always plays the greater role in most successes.

What many of us have failed to understand are the methods and opportunities that were available to those wealthy people. Are those opportunities still available now or are other opportunities available? Is it still possible these days that a company's stock as low as $10 per share can still rise to $50,000 per share? In what time frame is this still possible? What kinds of businesses should the company invest in to achieve this? These are questions the obsessed man never asks. He just hears of a business with a wonderful income and jumps in. There are internet users today who venture practically into all online money ventures they come across. I was a true victim of internet (online) business obsession for several years.

Many people will not chase the money directly but indirectly with the same obsessive vigor. Some people claim they will not do anything illegal to get money, but they can help finance a theft or scheme to defraud another person or entity! You cannot do anything for money but you can sponsor others to do anything for money, for a share in the profit! You still admire the money but you do not want to be linked to its source. What is really legal or illegal for this person?

The obsession to succeed will definitely drive you into illegalities that will aid scammers in scamming you. Many scam victims will claim the business was legitimate. If they would be honest with themselves here, they would admit that at one time or the other in the said business process, very clear manifestations of illegalities presented themselves, but they still carried on with the business because they wanted to succeed.

Do not think that you can hide all you desire. People easily know when you want something desperately or rather your actions easily expose what you want desperately. An American man was scammed $50,000 as bribe for government officials in Ghana to enable him secure an Airport renovation contract. Let me ask, what is the punishment for bribing a government official in the USA? He will not bribe officials in USA but he can bribe officials in Ghana. This creates a scammer's paradise.

The mentality you form about your immediate and far surroundings is crucial. Never think that others are fools or timid while you are clever. Never assume that you are more knowledgeable than your business partner because his or her English grammar (oral and written) is not good. Bear in mind that your spoken language might not be the mother tongue of your business partner. Bad grammatical errors do not mean naivety. Many people are not literate but they are very smart with 'native sense'. **Native sense** is the ability to make intelligent decisions and sound judgements without the benefits of formal education.

It is clear that scammers have native sense; they easily lure their unsuspecting victims into desperation and obsession, then they will capitalize on these. Native sense is very deceiving and a great advantage to those who have it. A man with native sense might appear not very educated or exposed, making his educated business partner assume, to be in charge or will surely be in charge. But in moments, the native sense man will use simple and common sense to debase the educated partner. The native sense man can achieve this feat easily as long as that ***obsession to succeed*** has been fully established in the educated man. Common sense is not so common after all.

A very deceiving aspect of money chasing is the ***"nearly"*** game. I prefer to call it money chasing because those involved are just following the money trail, which can take them to hell. They consider nothing else but following the track of big money-making like an obsession.

'I nearly concluded the business yesterday'.
'My money almost came yesterday but for . . . .'
'My money is due tomorrow'.
'Everything is okay and my payment should be paid next week'.
'I would have had $1million in my account yesterday if not for the . . . .'
'We almost got the money last week'.

'My money is due next week'.
'I nearly made $10,000,000 two days ago'.

The above 'nearly' episodes in money chasing are worrisome. Any business venture that always ends with *'nearly' (almost concluded)* and *then restarts again,* is not worthwhile and must be reconsidered unless you are gambling. Then, at least you know you are gambling where anything can happen. So many people who finally become scam victims are true believers of the 'nearly' game.

The *nearly* game is a major consideration in understanding most scams and it is always played where the victim is obsessed with succeeding or where it is obvious that the victim is a money chaser. The billing system scammers employ in their trade is systematic and very effective in not only extorting their victims, but also in creating that obsession to succeed in their victims. (See Chapter 20—*Systematic billing and Self billing in Scam businesses*)

Money chasing goes the distance—every now and then, you nearly got the breakthrough but you kept spending to get there. Do not mistake the 'nearly' game with an eventual business success borne out of several attempts or hard work. In a genuine business you might have been following the wrong approach and after several attempts you might have found a way to success. For instance, you might have been bidding for a contract without knowing your quote was on the high side, only for you to adjust it downwards and secure the contract. You might have taken your book manuscript to 50 publishers, only for the 51st publisher to publish it. They are all different from the scammer's 'nearly' game where you would have spent money for each quote submitted or you would have spent money for each publisher who considered your book. If you were spending on every step, then kindly reconsider or re-evaluate your agents or contacts. Foul play is present.

Now let us consider another aspect of money chasing. This kind of obsession and money chasing totally disorganizes the scam victim and is very difficult to correct, particularly when the victim involved is the secretive type. It is the *nearly* game of 'working for the scammer'.

Mr. Mathew had a serious business when he promised to buy his wife a new car. He reaffirmed this promise monthly, but three years later, he still had not bought the promised car. Mr. Mathew was in a

scam business where he lost over $200,000 to the scammers during the previous three years.

You will notice that Mr. Mathew could not have been making empty promises to his wife for three years. He must have had something coming, and buying a car for his beloved wife was the least he could do, but unfortunately for him, he was unknowingly involved in a scam characterized by the *nearly* game. By the time he realized it, $200,000 was gone and the promised car had not been bought. You might wonder how possible is this? This is very possible as a matter of fact. The scammers might have scammed Mr. Mathew out of $200,000 altogether, in several payments never exceeding $10,000 at a time, during the three years Mr. Mathew was in business with his scammers. The promised car was $30,000 and there was never a time when Mr. Mathew had a lump sum of $30,000 to buy his wife the promised car. Yet he lost $200,000. Scams can operate in this way or have this effect on the scam victims. Many are in same situation today; they have invested so much money in a business but cannot pay minor bills in the house.

Buying a $30,000 car for his wife was insignificant compared to what Mr. Mathew was expecting from the business into which he had invested $200,000. This is not a strange or a singular occurrence. Mr. Mathew was obsessed with succeeding in his business or he was keen on achieving business success that was so near (so close) for three good years. Mr. Mathew was obsessed with the success of whatever business he had.

Think of the possibility if Mr. Mathew had told the scammers that he was unable to make one of the payments because he needed to buy his wife a car, the scammers might have allowed him to do so? If Mr. Mathew could have done this, then he wouldn't have been committed to the scam business and might have lost less.

When one is obsessed with success in a business, nothing else will matter, except that business success making the 'nearly' game very effective in such situations. That is why a scam victim can be paying millions to the scammers while his or her family is scraping to put food on the table. There are gamblers in casinos that will quarrel and get very angry with casino waiters over the third serve of whiskey while they have just lost $10,000 in an hour that could have bought them a carton of the best whiskey. This attitude is common when one's judgment has been impaired or over ridden by the obsession to succeed and the overall effect of the scam by scammers and casinos alike.

It is common for someone chasing such success to forget the value of his or her chase after several end point attempts, without actually ending the chase. The closer you reached the end, the greater the desire for the next attempt to succeed. It is the *nearly* game that the scammers employ to perfection when dealing with victims who are obsessed with business success or with money chasing.

Nearly episodes have a way of making the chaser never to rethink the importance of the whole chase. It normally becomes an obsession with success. The chaser's priority becomes distorted; to record success in the chase but not the profit made from the chase.

Do not chase money aimlessly, allowing your sense of judgment, assessment and evaluation to be overtaken or overridden by the obsession to succeed in whatever you are chasing. ***You might end up losing something you will never get back, even if you get twenty times richer.***

CHAPTER 4

IMITATING SUCCESSFUL PERSONS

This is where I blame the successful man or woman. Over 70% of successful people tell their success stories, asserting that luck played the major role in their success. Some do this in order not to appear arrogant and show gratitude to God Almighty, others tell their success stories with emphasis on luck to show that others can also succeed in the same way or that it can also be done by another person—'The idea was nothing so special, I was lucky'.

Somehow, I still believe that if these wealthy people had told their success stories with more emphasis on hard work, which is exactly what it was, and less emphasis on luck, many people may not have been deceived today by scammers and conmen.

In a virtual success chart, an average person is a successful person such as a rich person is. The difference resides in the level of success. The same chart maintains that there are three components that must make success. They are Hard work, Skill and Luck. If God Himself rested after creation, then there was work. So, let us give Hard work 40%. Skill and Luck we give 30% each, because in an ideal society everyone should have equal opportunities or rather what every good society pursues. So, hard work makes 40%, skill 30% and luck 30% of a 100% success story. Now, the average person (one who has just enough, no excesses) needs 65% minimum score on this chart to make it while the rich person needs 75% score or more on this chart to be regarded as wealthy.

You can clearly deduce from the chart that a combination of all luck and skill (60%) can only draw you nearer to an average person (65%); you still need 5% hard work to be average. For one to be rich, a combination of these three components is a must. When you are very hardworking (40%) and well skilled (30%) you still remain in the average or high average level (70%), needing 5% luck in addition to be rich. The same is applicable to the very hardworking (40%) and very lucky (30%) person. Carefully, note that to even guarantee an average person's status when you are so skilled (30%) and swimming in luck (30%), hard work must come in; a minimum of 5% hard work to make 65%. Skill and hard work seem to move together—even when you have only skill—to exhibit that skill requires little hard work. Therefore, to guarantee riches above average, you must get a minimum of 5% luck at worst even if you have all the other attributes. An educated and well informed person (skill 30%), and very lucky (Luck 30%) still needs 5% hard work to be average and about 15% hard work to be very rich. Hard work can be achieved by several means; waking up in time, being in the office, going to work, dressing well, setting schedules, keeping appointments, doing your homework, and so on. Can one become an ace pilot without being a pilot? Can one win the New York state lottery without buying the tickets? Even in inheritance, there is some effort done.

The present day successful man, out of sentiment, over emphasizes his luck as the main attribute to his success. Sometimes the wrong notion is emphasized by the media or reporters. If you properly analyze success stories, you will discover that luck played not more than 30% of that rich person's success. Luck cannot be determined and comes in different forms with different impacts on different business transactions. Even where all the attributes of success are present, there must still be luck for real success to occur. Luck can be in the form of favorable government policies, honest workers, a good wife or husband, responsible children, no natural disasters, supportive bank officials, non greedy business partners, and so on.

The additional advantage with no calculated cost, apart from skill and hard work, is luck. Luck therefore is an advantage in success but never the main attribute.

Many people perceive luck wrongly. You will notice that the majority of success story listeners only take full notice or are only interested in the story part that deals with luck. The hard work part they disregard, claiming that several people today have done the same and are still struggling or barely making ends meet. They feel that the skill and hard work parts of success are for the business management experts and only hope for the luck part to come their way. They dream of such luck and pray earnestly for such luck. I insist that the three; hard work, skill and luck must be present for there to be success when defined as being wealthy.

A top Saudi Arabian business man lost $2 million to scammers in South Africa swayed by the notion that it was a similar kind of business in which his best friend in Brussels was involved, and which made him a billionaire. A communication mogul's friend lost a lot of money to scammers from Nigeria simply because his American communication friend told him that his communication business fortune came from his several money transfer businesses with top government officials in Nigeria.

Yes, so many corrupt world leaders and presidents of countries used contracts and contractors both within and outside their countries to siphon illegal funds for themselves. This does not mean that all such similar-looking businesses are true. Many are scams presented in similar styles.

Official corruption and financial misappropriation in many developed countries are illegal and often unheard of. Some business men in developed countries still believe that the easiest place to make their fortune is through the governments in Africa and in the developing world. The colonial masters came, took their share and left without anyone questioning their involvement, so why not them.

Mr. Kirkwood, a manufacturer, lost $500,000 to some scammers who pretended to be importers in West Africa. Mr. Kirkwood tried to export (dump) his products (toxic waste) into their country. His imagination must have told him that they would never know what he was shipping, but he was eager to help the scammers pay the relevant import duties in their country. To dispose of the waste in his country would have cost him $5 million or more, so he chose West Africa where, he supposed, people were ignorant. It was not so, eventually. Likewise, so many growing businesses in developing countries have lost all their business fortune to imaginary exporters in developed countries, which they saw or met on the internet. These young businesses made payments to those foreign firms for goods and have not heard a word from those firms to date. The worst is that the majority of these illiterate importers do not know how to go about recovering their losses or locating these foreign firms.

The real situation is that everything has changed; because it worked for Mr. A does not mean it will work for Mr. B. Mr. A might have been lucky to succeed while Mr. B would lose a fortune doing same business. Every business situation is unique and must be judged from its specific perspective and never from the perspective of another. Scam and fraud are everywhere these days and there are no exceptions.

If we may divide luck (30%) into three parts (10%). Those who hope for more than 10% luck are always open to scams. Out of the three main uncontrollable advantages that will make your business successful, always plan and pray for one part out of the three to come true and it should be enough to realize your business. Better put; always plan your business in such a way that 10% luck should be able to realize your business. If two parts (20%) of luck or more come through, then you can become the next very rich person.

I once invested in a HYIP that looked very real. The investments had three levels. My suspicion about it remained strong as my main worry was when the HYIP would vanish, if it was a scam. I split my luck into three parts. I invested $100 on a 20% return. After three days my balance was $120. I quickly accepted my first part of 10% luck and withdrew all my $120 saying goodbye to the HYIP. The HYIP kept advertising their second and third stages to me for over a month through emails which I ignored. Later, this same HYIP fleeced other people of larger amounts. These people went for the second and third stage investments that promised to pay more than 50%.
I hoped for only 10% luck and when it came, I was satisfied.

Do not imitate success stories; times vary and conditions differ. Science, technology and IT has made it possible to easily present similar business conditions these days to lure anyone into scams. They look similar, sound real, but are neither similar nor real.
If the successful friend you wish to imitate is possibly a good friend, try to acquaint him or her with the details of your own business. You will be surprised at his or her reaction. How many of us will give our supposedly successful friend details of our new business venture when we secretly want to out shine him or her? Moreover, how many of our successful friends will take the time to tell us, step by step, how he or she

achieved outward success. These are human nature, scammers seem to understand.

Most common success story can be mere assumptions and not reality.

'She was so lucky that her business partner left the whole money to her . . . 'How sure are you that this is the real story of her success?

'He was very lucky to make it big by selling his gold during the recession . . . 'You forgot that he must have made effort to save his gold during the boom.

Many people prefer the upper part and never consider the lower part of the two examples above, and that is why the scammer is still thriving in his or her trade.

Believe it; every scammer in any scam is imitating one, two or a combination of similar genuine business processes or transactions. *The scammer's advantage is the imitation of genuine processes his or her victim cannot accurately evaluate.*

CHAPTER 5

THE OLD PHENOMENON

One of the main factors in deception is distraction. Distraction has been part of life itself and it moves hand in hand with deception.

Scammers seem to have modified distraction by first presenting a pronounced benefit to their scam target. Normally, in most deceptions, a benefit is offered which clouds the victim's vision and forces him or her to ignore what is being taken from him or her. This practice has always existed as far back as history has been recorded, and will continue to thrive. Exploitation, slave trade, and colonialism, all began with an initial giving before the massive taking. The giving can even be an act of simple kindness, but it comes first before any taking.

The Initial Giving: The initial giving makes it hard for you to bother with the later takings. An initial act of kindness, generosity, honesty, favor, admission, etc., whatever it takes to soften the ground, take the bite out of a future request or simply create distraction, are the weapons of the scammer.

The ancient Chinese call it *'giving before you take'*.

Another theory implies; *'When asking for help, appeal to the person's self interest, and never to their mercy or gratitude'. More capable people will assist you for what they will gain themselves, than out of pity for your plight.*

Scammers employ these weapons in their scam proposals. In seeking the alliance with an unsuspecting target in a scam proposal, the scammer carefully implants what the target stands to get. Often, the scammer will blow this gain out of proportion, but the fact remains that the scammer makes it clear what the scam target stands to gain if he or she cooperates. It is a fact that scam targets tend to respond better to proposals (scam proposals) when they perceive something to be gained for themselves.

'The shortest and best way to make your fortune is to let people perceive clearly that it is in their interests to promote yours' (Jean de La Bruyere, 1645-1696).

A beautiful business venture with a lot to gain is normally attractive. Most people never ask why you want to make them rich. Few ask without answers, but they still proceed with the business. Some forms of scams do not create room for asking these questions, as is common on the internet. All details, processes and gains are carefully explained on the website and all you need to do is register for you to be in the scam. No questions and no answers until you have invested, and then you can get a 24-hour customer service, still depending on your investment level! The majority of the provided answers cannot be authenticated; they are neither here nor there.

It is as old as time that most deceptive proposals contain an 'offer'. The *offer* is something desirable. The deceiver will normally present the offer in a way to enhance a 'sale of confidence'. ***Sale of confidence*** is that initial goodwill not currently earned. Informing you on a goodwill you have not earned—To have been remembered out of a whole lot of people can arouse a serious sense of self-importance in anyone. The scammer's proposal does not miss to create these impressions for his or her scam target. Scammer will claim all kinds of things in showcasing their offers and sales of confidence.

Some words used by scammers are:
'Trust in your ability to assist me';
'Your professional suitability';
'Confiding in you';
'A strictly confidential business';
'Faith in your uprightness not to cheat me'.

The offer and Sale of Confidence are two major scam tactics that prompt responses from unsuspecting scam targets. They are the traits of a scam business proposal. They will be discussed again in features of scam businesses, Part 3.

So, the phenomenon of scammers first offering something to take later is as old as anything, but so many eventual scam victims never realized when the offer was made. Every scam has a proposal containing something the scam target stood to gain if he or she went into the business. Even when the scammer tries to beat about the bush in making the proposal sound genuine, there is still an inbuilt offer in the proposal.

This phenomenon as old as it is still appears in all scams today. For those who do not believe it; is like believing that miracles only happened in Jesus' time. Miracles still happen every day and will continue to happen tomorrow and the next day. The only difference resides in what we considered miracles yesterday are no longer miracles today, and even greater miracles today might not be regarded as miracles tomorrow.

If you have ever received scam proposals, go back to them now, you will notice that each of them had an offer no matter how it was presented. Even in situations, where genuine business became scam, the offer sneaked in, so the victim could not locate its intrusion. Another fact is that the majority of eventual scam victims would not have gone into the business (scam business) if it had not been for what they stood to gain.

It is important that serious effort be made to locate the offer in any business proposal.

Offers in business proposals should not be seen as desired benefits you have to reciprocate as the business progresses.

The sale of confidence to the scam target (prospective victim) is initially, 'goodwill not earned', but when the scam victim reciprocates the confidence in the scammer, the scam victim will always feel the scammer has earned it, due to the initial giving from the scammer.

This is the old game scam targets, prospective victims and scam victims ought to understand.

CHAPTER 6

SCAM STAGE SETTINGS

People hardly realize when they walk into a scam stage. It is on a virtual stage that scamming occurs. The scam stage is set virtually like a normal drama stage for the scam to be successful. Such as on a drama stage, where sitting arrangements, lightings, acting materials etc., are placed on the stage for acting a drama, a scam stage is set with the prospective victim and the scammer providing all of the necessary acting conditions for the scam to be acted out. The majority of scam stages can be set knowingly or unknowingly, but the scammer always performs his scam on a set stage.

Scam is defined as a clever and dishonest plan for making money. A plan meaning something you intend to do or achieve—bear in mind that the detail processes have been well considered in advance. On the one hand, the scammer has already calculated his or her various moves, waiting for the scam target's entrance into an already set stage. On the other hand, the scammer can easily detect a set stage and take full advantage of it.

Scam is a game because it has a winner and a loser. Where a scam fails, genuine business might ensue or we will consider it a draw because the scammer might have lost nothing tangible. I have also noticed that real businesses ensue when you are very careful or scam proof in your dealings with a supposed scammer; the supposed scammer will either deal genuinely with you or claim it is out of stock.

The scammer has a detail well considered plan, the ***primary plan*** being to extort monetary gains or other gains from the prospective victim. The ***secondary plan*** is how the scammer will execute these extortions on the prospective victim which is prone to changes depending on the prospective victim's nature, attitude and character. Yet the primary plan (objective) to extort the prospective victim remains intact.

Scam stages are numerous; some scam stages are set by the scammer awaiting the victim's entrance while other scam stages are set unknowingly by the victims. Scammers try to set their own scam stages but can also take full advantage of already set scam stages. For instance, a scam proposal sent to a scam target via any communication medium can be a scam stage set by the scammer while desperation for something can be a scam stage set unknowingly by the scam target. If a manufacturer produces inferior goods that spoil easily and buyers keep coming back to buy new ones, are those buyers being scammed? If somebody sold something inferior to you and was willing to give back a 90% refund, has the seller scammed you?

A secretary working in a recruiting office secretly told some applicants who came for interview that she will be able to assist them in securing the job for $500 each. She said the $500 will be for gratification purposes to some of the interviewing officials. Some applicants asked what if she did not help in securing the job after the $500 payment. She replied, 'You know how these things are but at worst you will get $400 back. Out of desperation many accepted and paid $500. Two weeks later the applicants checked in and there was no employment to be secured. They were all very happy when the secretary returned the $400 balance to each of them.

Probably, the secretary did nothing exceptional to help, but she made $1800 out of the 18 applicants who bought her idea. She simply sampled her proposal and 18 applicants bought it. She may have simply kept their money in her drawer to retrieve it two weeks later and deduct her $100 from each applicant. Do not be surprised if such an interview was set up from the outset to scam these applicants. Of course, it will initially appear genuine due to the vacancy notice, but it was a scam nonetheless. Maybe those applicants should have said 'use all $500 and get me the job or return all $500!' This sounds improper and indecent from someone desperately expecting a job. Yet it might have been the right thing to say in such circumstances. The secretary's proposal was very clear; she was merely after the $100, but how many applicants thought of it in the midst of all the interview staging?

The main thing here is that some business stages are prone to scam, and most common scenarios can be converted to scam stages by the scammers. It might have been conceived at the outset or conceived during the business process. Whatever the business, you are communicating with an objective in mind and you are playing a game to achieve your objectives. Your attitude, requests, actions, moves and even what you say has the potential to demonstrate your final objective in the eyes of a close observer. One who is careful could not have fallen for that secretary's plot. Either the job or $500 full refund should have been the case.

Let us observe closely other business stages that can mature into scam stages.

Mr. Gabs was a business man who visited Düsseldorf on a business trip to buy second hand cars for resale. In Düsseldorf, he met Mr. Mahmud, a second-hand car exporter based in that city. Known only to Mr. Mahmud, he was willing to sell a mixture of stolen and low-grade cars to Mr. Gabs. Mr. Mahmud showed Mr. Gabs his cars at give-away prices. Mr. Gabs claimed that his funds for payment were still coming, having sent them through telegraphic transfer. The stage was set. With all seriousness, Mr. Gabs ensured that Mr. Mahmud followed him to the bank where he was expecting his incoming wire transfer. Sensing he had the sale secured, Mr. Mahmud started assisting Mr. Gabs with meals, accommodation, bills, etc. Mr. Mahmud also made sure that Mr. Gabs did not interact with other second-hand car dealers or anyone else who might jeopardize his scheme of selling his 'design' second hand cars to Mr. Gabs. After ten good days of spending close to $3,000 on Mr. Gabs' meals, accommodation, sightseeing, etc., Mr. Mahmud was forced again to ask Mr. Gabs about the incoming money transfer; Mr. Gabs had no answer and insisted they returned to the bank. This time the bank advised that they should contact the transferring bank, which they did promptly. The transferring bank in Mr. Gabs' country then insisted that Mr. Gabs returned home to complete the transfer papers personally. So, Mr. Gabs had to leave and said he would be back in two days. Mr. Gabs never came back to Düsseldorf.

This is a scenario many people easily run into and get scammed. Mr. Mahmud set his business perfectly. Unfortunately he could not assess Mr. Gabs and was too quick in chasing the 'offer' for his kind of business. Mr. Gabs might have never had any money coming to him, Mr. Mahmud should not have started paying for Mr. Gab's meals and accommodation without being sure that Mr. Gabs' funds were in fact coming or already deposited in the bank account. Mr. Mahmud set the stage for him to be scammed out of $3,000. Maybe Mr. Gabs came for sightseeing and wanted Mr. Mahmud to pay his expenses. All Mr. Mahmud needed to do was to assure Mr. Gabs that he would start working on his orders as soon as his funds arrived, or as soon as a deposit was made. If this had been the case, then a draw would have ensued. In a draw, Mr. Mahmud would allow Mr. Gabs to do his homework on buying second-hand cars and he might have known the real prices and maybe they would have gone into business together.

Scams are complicated. It is very complex at times to pinpoint the real target of the scammer, the presentation might differ but the final objective is your money; in this case, paying for Mr. Gab's expenses.

Let us look at another simple scam stage that is set on a daily basis.

Mr. Adam and Mr. Ben are both traveling to the same conference outside the state with their cars.

Mr. Adam drives into a garage and tells the mechanic **'please check my car, I need to travel with it'**.

Likewise at a different time, Mr. Ben drives into the same garage and tells the mechanic, **'I want my car in full order'**.

Mr. Adam and Mr. Ben both want their cars fit for travel but their statements could lead to different interpretations, if the mechanic is a fraudster. Irrespective of who is doing the right thing needed for such a journey, Mr. Ben has exposed himself more to a possible scam, while Mr. Adam has restricted his exposure to a possible scam by the mechanic.

The way you make a request, act or present anything sometimes determines the meaning perceived from it. Carelessly, you can easily expose your ignorance or knowledge level about something, creating room for a scam to take place. The car mechanic will be specific in fixing Mr. Adams' car to enable him to travel, it might be brakes and or tires which he will check and fix. For Mr. Ben, the mechanic will perceive a situation where Mr. Ben has enough money to fix everything in his car, including imaginary works. Mr. Ben has just manufactured bills for himself by his statement and will definitely be billed systematically, while Mr. Adam just restricted his exposure to scam by his statement.

Remember, the car mechanic knows best for your car when you drive into his garage. *What one does not know will remain so until he or she is directly or indirectly taught, or experienced it.*

When the news broke that a top Brazilian banker lost about $250 million to scammers, it was unbelievable. Some scams are very advanced. It is sad that a man of such banking status lacked the elementary know-how to detect that some percentage of the business was a scam. He could have lost a million or two and detected the scam, but to have lost $250 million without noticeable suspicion was unpardonable and a show of gross misconduct on the part of a top banker with all his banking experiences. Irrespective of the scammer's manipulation skills, the said business processes must have presented scam features. Either he did not notice them or he totally misinterpreted them. Also, apart from the scammer's settings, the scam stage used in this huge scam must have been a mega scam stage that had photographers (insiders), stage directors (prompters) and editors (financial institutions) who were scammers too. Some scam stages have such affiliations.

The new globalization is a perfect stage for scams, so everyone must be careful. So many scam stages are emerging daily. You must remain articulate and have your readymade test kit for all business proposals. I mean *all* proposals. You will be approached with these get-rich-quick offers via the internet, mail, emails, telephone and even face-to-face meetings. At times the proposal might even come from somebody you know very well, who might not know what he or she is being used for. They are all games designed to have you part with your money willingly. The amount is irrelevant; most victims only realized it was a scam when the game was over and they had no more money to finance further expenses for the business (scam). Some victims lose a few dollars, some thousands or millions. A scam is a product that has no fixed price. The amount lost in a scam transaction, in most successful scam cases, is what the scam victim had access to. Yes, if the victim had access to more funds, he or she could have lost more unless the victim knew or realized it was a scam and stopped paying. The Brazilian banker mentioned above stopped paying because he could not get more funds from the bank; his funding source. Questions were being asked and it was then he realized it was a scam and the police came in. The funniest thing about a scam is that you can never recover the whole amount lost, no matter the kind of police you employ, no matter what is seized from the scammers. Some scammed funds just cannot be recovered. An example is the bank charges that were applied during transfers and retransfers of the funds.

A scam stage can be set anywhere, even in legitimate businesses employing legitimate people. It has been observed that some advanced fraudsters now use bank transfer fees and charges as a well-devised scam, while they refund the balance after these numerous bank deductions. This advanced scam method is becoming frequent when the right scam stage is set. The scam stage here is to lure you to make the payment first, which now enters into the transfer and retransfer mediums to return to the original owner not complete. Bear in mind that the banks and institutions deducting these charges are owned by human beings who seek profit in business, too. Legal practitioners are also getting involved in this advanced scam claiming legal fees. One avoiding scam must now understand that, even the courts know that thieves need lawyers, who might get paid with the stolen money in question.

Business is influencing others to give you their money or services. Manufacturers persuade you to give them your money while selling their products; a service man does the same while servicing your various needs. In life, we keep trying to get others to agree with us every day. People come across scam stages often; at times you escape unknowingly without making a real effort to avoid them. Sometimes your knowledge (wisdom) can be ignorance elsewhere, and walk you directly onto a scam stage.

A very wealthy French man received a letter proposing a business transaction that would benefit him to the tune of $55 million. The proposer (scammer) claimed he knew the French man at the University of California. The French man not remembering clearly and suspecting foul play asked the proposer which year and which accommodation he was in campus. Wise! The scammer did a little research, replying with the appropriate answers and explanations. In turn the French man let his guard down and entered into the business transaction whole heartedly—trust scam. In the business that ensued, the French man lost close to $3 million.

The above scam stage was based on trust of old friends from the University of California. The French man's questions are very easy to answer as long as universities continue to post and advertise their facilities on the internet. The scammer's paradise is a trust scam stage. Whenever a scam target enters a 'trust' scam stage, then a good percentage of the scam proposal's sale of confidence is already done.

Much effort must be exerted to detach such scam victim from such scam stage, if he or she entered a trust scam stage. Trust scams are very effective because you believe that your partners or prompters cannot deceive you. What the French man did not know was that their alumni magazine was intercepted by a Paris scammer, who now pretended to be an alumnus. The French man thought there was no way he would know campus details without being an alumnus. All these assumptions were wrong because of the internet and globalization. Two years into the business, the French man's younger brother, an MBA graduate, came into the business, too. Wiser, the younger brother put down a condition: he would not pay a cent unless he received the $55 million in his brother's account. The scammers changed their tactic, showing him a box in Paris containing the said money that needed only cleaning. Cleaning chemicals, powder, etc., and the brother put in another $1 million before realizing it was a scam. He quickly ran to the police authorities, Interpol was involved. The scammers had no face, no identity, only telephone numbers and fax numbers. The address they used in Paris was irregular as they drove the scam victim there. The police authorities were forced to remind the French men that they should have known at the outset that there could never be a $55 million cash business in such an environment where they went to collect the cash payment. 'How dare you invest $4 million in a business project based on just papers, documents and files sent via email and facsimile, plus a dilapidated location in Paris'?

The scam stage is one of the most important factors in any scam.

Deductions and analyses of several successful scams have shown that, what the scammer achieves by sending the scam proposal to any scam target is to set a stage (drama) based on falsehood.

Scammers also take advantage of set stages of which their victims are not aware, but which suit their scams.

Spread a rumor in your neighborhood that you want to buy a good second hand Lexus SUV. Such actions can set serious scam stages, not only for you but for others who have learned of your desperation for a Lexus SUV.

CHAPTER 7

THE CYBERSPACE

Cyberspace is the imaginary place where electronic data goes. It is that notional realm in which electronic information such as email, data, internet, etc., exists or is exchanged. The world is presently witnessing a developed cyberspace and with it has come many new crimes aptly named cyber and computer crimes. Irrespective of the advantages gained from the developed cyberspace, we must also understand the crimes associated with it.

Cyber crime is defined as any crime committed over a computer network. Cyber crime is also a term used for attacks perpetrated against the cyber security of business organizations, which can have several goals. The main goal pursued by criminals who perpetrate these crimes is to gain unauthorized access to their victims' private information. Computer crime is often used in tandem with cyber crime and refers to any crime that involves a computer and a network. Cyber crime and computer crime are both related to internet crimes, which also appears as internet scams.

Cyberspace has opened new frontier for these crimes, which the police and authorities must be aware of. These days, with many businesses being totally dependent on their proprietary computer data, cyber crimes have become more rampant. Many cyber criminals gain access to vital information on companies and individuals which they can *use directly to benefit themselves, sell to other criminals (including scammers) or use to inflict damage to that company or individual.* It is common for cyber criminals to use their extracted information as they wish. There have been cases where such information was modified or even deleted for their economic advantage or otherwise.

Cyber criminals can be external or internal. A good majority of cyber crimes occur within the same entity, for the same purpose; either using the information for their own benefit, selling or using the extracted information to inflict damage to the entities against which these cyber attacks were perpetrated. There are many disgruntled workers and employees in many organizations who commit most cyber crimes, selling data and facilitating the leakage of personal details on their companies' customers. The intent behind these disgruntled employees' crimes can be profit-oriented or damage-oriented. Moreover, such disgruntled employees are unable to control or determine the use of such extracted information once leaked out. I have come to the conclusion that many workers do these crimes simply to make more money.

Cyber crimes can also be associated with white-collar crimes. White-collar crimes are crimes committed by the upper class members of society who are normally wealthy, highly educated and legitimately employed. These socially connected white-collar criminals commit these crimes by non-physical means, employing concealment or deception. White-collar criminals use their positions to release vital information or data to other criminals who use the information in very dishonest fashions. The desire for more money should never be underestimated when checking who is engaged in criminal behavior. Most cyber crimes are motivated by greed and the prospect of financial gain rather than any other motive such as power, lust, revenge or adventure, etc.

IT equipment thefts, voluntary and involuntary release of vital information have all aided cyber crimes. *Hacking*, as a matter of fact, is the most commonly reported computer crime incident. A computer user who gains unauthorized access to a computer system or data belonging to someone else from an internal or external source is a hacker. It is common for firms to be very cautious about their external hacker protection while putting fewer emphases on their internal hacker protections.

At times I wonder how scammers and deceivers got certain private, personal information. Information is ultimate; the importance of information and the role it plays in businesses should never be underestimated. A good business person knows that good information represents money and leads to success. In a globalized world, information and data will rule; one with information definitely has a great advantage over others. Email lists are hotcakes on sale and new websites are being set-up daily for the sole purpose of gathering email addresses to make up email lists to sell to anyone who needs them. Considering these developments and cyber crimes themselves, *it is very important that anyone wishing to avoid scams must not ignore the roles played by cyberspace criminals in facilitating many scams and frauds.*

A close observation will indicate that *the number of junk mails (plus scam proposals) an internet user receives as email is directly proportional to the number of websites that internet user visits or interact with.* The more websites you visit whether completing registration forms or interacting, the greater the number of junk mails and scam mails you will be receiving in your inbox. This happens regularly, regardless of all the clear notices from those visited websites that they will not sell you information nor use your information illegally. Even newly opened email addresses that are just hours old still receive junk mail and scam proposals.

Now, how many people try to really check how their information leaked? The majority of us will simply ignore such junk mail (scam proposal) but the possibility that one day you might eventually come across a proposal that might interest you is there, as long as such emails keep accessing your email address.

I often wonder what would be the monetary value of all the email addresses in AOL, Google, Yahoo, Facebook, Twitter or Hotmail, to mention only a few. The monetary value of such data should definitely run into millions. I have come across—High Yield Investment Program (HYIP)—web designers' adverts; that were also selling 100,000 email addresses of previous investors in similar HYIPs. For a HYIP scammer, sending scam HYIP proposals to 100,000 email addresses is worthy, because, there must be responses. On the other hand, imagine the possibilities of what a scammer can do with 100,000 credit card information hacked from reputable firms with good customers.

The possibilities of what a cyber criminal can do with the extracted information (stolen information) are infinite. The extracted information can be used rightly or wrongly depending on who comes across it or rather who needs it. Information extracted by cyber criminals can be bought by genuine firms and used to enhance their products and service marketing. Likewise scammers easily come across such extracted information which will aid their scam proposals.

Grooming is one of the main attribute of scammers, as they try to establish a relationship with their prospective victim that will enable the scamming eventually. In establishing such preparatory scamming relationship with their unsuspecting victim, extracted information on the victim is always an added advantage.

I have always tried to make people understand that their private details did not just get to a scammer mysteriously; someone, somewhere, must have provided such information to the scammer knowingly or unknowingly. The problem in properly analyzing the leakage of such information resides in locating the exact leakage point. An employee in an Australian firm data section can provide his or her company customers' data to scammers in Senegal. The scammer in Senegal can sell some of the same data to another scammer in Alaska, USA. The latter will be calling scam targets and prospective victims from Alaska, making it difficult to pinpoint the exact leakage point of such data. Moreover, for many of us who interacts with many websites, it is more difficult to pinpoint the exact leakage point.

For instance; you submitted your personal information to a job recruitment website in Dubai, which is eventually provided to cyber criminals or hacked. Scammers in Canada can come across such extracted information, calling you from Canada with astonishing details about you. The Canadian scammer now has the required information to tailor his or her scam proposal to suit you accurately with a high success rate, because the information extracted from the job recruitment firm in Dubai was readily available.

Apart from tailoring specific scams to scam targets and prospective victims, information extracted by cyber criminals can also be used to set up other perfect scam stages for scam targets. A common example is seen in some job interviews where job applicants end up entering into another scam of a totally different nature while supposedly attending a job interview.

It is therefore important to be cautious when interacting with websites and to know exactly which private detail you want to share. *What ever information you share will eventually be used in trying to scam you when cyber criminals lay hands on that information.* When I separated my website interacting email address from my personal email address, I discovered a significant decrease in the junk emails and scam proposals I receive in my personal inbox.

It is evident that a good number of internet users easily interact with most websites they come across on the internet, providing their private details while filling out application or registration forms, which is not right.

CHAPTER 8

UNDERSTANDING GAINS AND LOSSES

Many people have miscalculated what is loss and what is gain in relation to doing business. What is business and what is gain in doing business? These are being misinterpreted, exposing many people to scams. It is very important in avoiding scams that the real quantification of gains and losses is well understood. If one spends $200 to discover that your new business venture is a scam, did you gain or lose? It is important to realize that you gained. The $200 spent might have saved you from absolute ruin. A successful business person spends money on risk management. If it will cost you something to know the truth is better than being ignorant.

After Mrs. Karl accepted to assist in the charity business (a scam), she got a new telephone line ($200) for the business, she also bought a fax machine ($300) and sent her charity firm letter headed papers by special courier ($150) to the scammer. Her suspicion that the said business was a scam continued to increased as the business progressed. Finally, she was able to buy a publication ($25) that clearly confirmed her doubts. She stopped the business and cancelled all further communications with the scammer.

Mrs. Karl might have wasted $650 previously but the $25 she spent in getting better information is invaluable and the gain supersedes the $650 she spent elsewhere, not even on the scammer. Permit me to say that in reality, she just gained a million dollars by buying that $25 publication. Considering the rate at which she was going, she could have set a record in the scam victims' list.

In avoiding scams you must accurately assess your gains and losses. If you assess gains and losses wrongly, a problem will definitely arise. You might start chasing your losses and end up losing more or getting scammed further. The majority of prospective victims and victims alike take this lightly and it is always a problem. You must appreciate the present value of what you have gained and the present value of what you have lost to be able to avoid scams. You must evaluate losses and gains correctly because the future in a scam business is unknown. The future of Mrs. Karl's bourgeois charity business was neither here nor there because it was a scam. It is possible that Mrs. Karl could have lost a million dollars or more to the scammers if not for the God sent $25 publication.

What is wrong in formally purchasing information, doing further research, approaching a private detective, an accountant or a financial adviser to help you check your new business venture? They are the right things to do, but most people consider the cost and confidentiality oath instead. As a good business person, you must have that time to do your research and cross check all information available to you before venturing into a new business. It might cost you a few dollars but when compared to what you could have lost otherwise, the few dollars were well worth it. The cost might even be only time, phone calls, office visit, web search, fact books, etc. Spending a little money or making a serious effort to verify business claims is always a gain, and not verifying business claims is always a loss, eventually.

An internet get rich scheme should have a telephone number that works. Do you know that most people only discover that the telephone numbers of such schemes do not work after investing money in the scheme without returns? Very funny! Something that should have been checked first is now being checked last. The majority of High Yield Investment Program (HYIPs) accepts only certain online payments because of reasons best known to them. Perfect Money, Liberty Reserve, Paypex, PayPal, Moneybookers, Bitcoin, and ClickandBuy to mention a few are all online payment solutions. It is now left for you to check the policies of these online payment solution firms to have a guide. Stop being lazy and make efforts to check this out, it might provide you enough information to know which online payment method is reliable and which can guarantee a refund should things go wrong. A detailed check will show that some online payment solution firms take scams and refunds seriously while other online payment solutions firms do not, and payments through them are as good as lost, should the business not materialize. You must know these things. A man who tells you that he is a president's son is not impossible to verify? Embassies, factbooks, detectives, are all there to assist you in checking these claims, at worst for a fee. In the process of checking anyone's claims, you will discover that your instinct will advise further on what to ask the claimer for more verification. It works like magic.

The cost of checking all these information may be negligible compared to what one might lose in a scam, if you do not check these things thoroughly. At times it is laziness which cannot be tolerated in the bid to avoid scams.

Another problem is that a good number of people being scammed are even afraid of hearing the truth. *'No matter how it is considered, knowing the truth is the greatest gain in anything'*.

Whether the truth is bad or good, it is always the best. Some victims of scams might not want to hear the truth; this is noticeable from their secrecy, their actions and their reactions. There is nothing wrong in listening to anyone with any information, the listener, if well informed, should have confidence in his or her judgment on what has been said, and on which position to adopt.

A good friend of mine in Holland was involved in about three scams simultaneously. Two were in Ghana and one in Nigeria. It all started when he called me one evening to assist him in sending $400 to an army officer in Nigeria. Without any suspicion, I really wanted to help him, so I called his business partner who refused to give me a bank account, telling me that I must send the money by Western Union. I became very suspicious and decided to help my friend further. On my insistence, my friend sent me all the correspondences and transaction details for these people, both in Nigeria and Ghana, which I studied thoroughly, and without doubt, concluded they were definite scammers. My friend had already spent close to $2 million on the businesses. I then took the time to explain to my friend that these people were scammers, with enough evidence and references to back my claim. I even gave him the direct telephone numbers of those government agencies he thought he was dealing with. I begged him to verify my observations, and urged him to stop dealing with these scammers. He responded that I was making a mistake, that he met the Army General in Nigeria when he was executing a contract at the Kaduna refinery, had known the General for over six years before he met me in Amsterdam and that there was no way the General could be a fraudster. At this stage, I knew what the problem was.

He was deep in the scam and he was not willing to believe otherwise. He just could not bear the truth so he did not want to hear it. I pitied him, so I continued trying to save him. At times he would not answer my calls for weeks or reply to my emails, but I made it my duty to forward any available information to him as soon as one was within reach. I asked him how a Major General in the army could be asking for $400 as wire charges to send my friend $7 million. The General could simply deduct $400 from the money and send him the balance. My friend thought, I did not want to help him. He even pleaded with me to send the $400 via Western Union to the Major General, if I really wished him well. I did not send anything, because I knew it was a pure waste and an insult to my knowledge. I used every means available to me in trying to convince him but it was very hard. A while later, my friend opened up a little, and I was able to deduce that it had been an ongoing scam of over invoiced contract sum at the Kaduna refinery. I invited him to Nigeria for a one-on-one explanation but he rejected my invitation. He said he had never been to Nigeria in his whole life, yet initially, he had been bold enough to tell me he knew the Major General in Nigeria when he was executing a contract. You can now understand the effect of a scam. My friend was not only believing the brainwashing the scammer had done on him but he was now manufacturing lies to satisfy his belief in a business he cannot bear to admit was a scam. I have no doubt that in his mind, he believed there was $7 million and the money was his.

My friend gave the only thing he would have gained no chance. The truth would have been his only gain in this whole business that has taken him years. He gradually put me aside and I am sure he is still in the businesses or he would have replied to the emails I sent months ago. This attitude is pure characteristics of a deeply committed scam victim.

I also believe that these attitudes by scam victims can be psychological. For the majority, their commitments so far cannot allow them to believe they have just wasted their time and money. You simply spoil their day when they find out that the big business is not real or the guy is not the president's son as he claimed, instead of being very happy.

For some;

'Where there is life, there is hope'.

For others;

'Where there is hope, there is life'.

It is common for a scam victim to live in hope that the business would materialize, which will never happen. People vary; some people get scammed and when they discover it was a scam, they stop further expenditure, change their contacts, avoid further scams, re-focus on reality and bear the loss, putting the whole thing down to a bad experience. They still achieve new successes elsewhere. The second group of people wakes up strong, fresh, articulate, agile and happy as long as they believe that a certain business venture, in which they will make millions of dollars, is still on schedule. The consideration that the venture still has not materialized is secondary to them.

Commitment is an inhibitor in understanding gains and losses in any business. Commitment is what harms the scam victim. Commitment penetrates your mind and negates your logical thinking; the more you believe in something and repeat that belief continually, the more your subconscious will recognize it as truth. You can even go extra lengths to certify this truth. This is what happens to many victims of scams. It gets to a stage where they firmly believe the promised gain is actually coming to them. They move forward and without remembering the business's origin anymore, they invest heavily in it—literally blindfolded to the truth. ***If only a scam victim can ignore the ongoing business processes and remember how it all started, he or she might be able to decipher if the present business is a scam.*** Only acknowledging the truth can remove the commitments entirely, in a scam business.

When scam victims have been fully committed, it is easier for a scammer to introduce scam occultism which will grossly inhibit the scam victim's assessment skill. ***Scam occultism*** is the use of dangerous code of **secrecy**, magic, witchcraft and spirits in scam business manipulations. Scam occultism is a dangerous end game that can go any way; it can be used to extort further money from the scam victims and it can be used to discharge the scam victims without their complaining. It can also lead to very dangerous societal crimes. The confidentiality treaty in scams (secrecy) and occultism are related. (See Chapter 23—*Scam Occultism and the Secrecy*)

No one in a secret setting can properly assess gains and losses in that setting.

Anything done in secret is for the gain of few and never for all.

The scammer employs business secrecy to play this role. When you cannot tell anyone else about the business, including your loved ones, then you have been properly initiated into the cult. Secrecy, as a tool in inhibiting assessment of gain and losses, has worked on a great percentage of scam victims. This same effect is applicable in societal cults; as a member of a secret cult, you can never be able to assess your gains and losses in that cult. You are only open to the manipulation of the cult leaders. The police are fully aware of this fact. To be able to assess your gains and losses, you must first break the oath of secrecy. Telling someone else about your 'wonderful' business, even loved ones might be the magic wand that will rescue you finally from the scam business in which you have been involved.

There are so many fake websites on the internet, you must also be careful in contacting police to assist in recovering lost funds in scan businesses. Some scam victims ended up losing more money in trying to recover the previous loss, simply because they did not know that the trusted officers they were contacting by email or phone were the same scammers in another form or new scammers entirely. There are cases where the same scammers impersonate the police, making you believe that they will help you in recovering your losses and in arresting the culprits. Past commitments easily induce most scam victims to engage in these further mistakes. Most scam victims will jump at any possible solution made available to them to recover their lost money and they end up falling right back into the scammers' hands again. In many case studies, the frequent new payments requests, scam victims have to pay this 'police' assisting them in recovering their lost money should be enough to inform such scam victims on who is the police and who is not.

Summarily, if you are sure it is a scam, cease spending more and report to the authorities in person and not by email or fax. Consider yourself lucky—as one who just won the million dollar lottery. Try to disregard your past losses, calculate the present gain represented by the new information and knowledge that the business was a scam. ***Do not even spend a cent further on anybody or police, no matter what.*** If you can curtail further expenses of any kind in that very business then you have started recovering.

Many have argued that keeping quiet after being scammed is cowardice. My point of view is analyzing the worth of keeping quiet against the worth of reacting. Every actions performed in a *confirmed* scam business must be quantified properly. In Part 4 Chapter 27, we look at the laws on scam and frauds. Meet a legal professional in person to know where your case stands or could stand. Consider all aspects thoroughly before leaving all you should be doing for the future to chase the past.

Let us look at this story in '48 Laws of Power'.

Mr. J Frank Norfleet spent 5 years hunting con artists and successfully, he single-handedly tracked them down and destroyed the country's largest confederation of con artists in America. The effort bankrupted him, ruined his marriage and his life. They said he died a satisfied man.

Such men exist but I prefer the "once beaten twice shy" theory. Anyone can be conned, scammed or fooled. No one is above a con. Con has been there since time immemorial. Great men, great women, personalities have been scammed, likewise, kings, lords, and presidents. Do not allow being conned, scammed or fooled to activate your self-doubt and make you desperate to repair any damage to your integrity. It is a clear sign of insecurity.

Let us check the gains and losses for Mr. Norfleet. Was his bankruptcy, the collapse of his marriage and his ruined life worth the revenge over his embarrassment in being fleeced? Please note that overcoming your embarrassment is not worth any price.

The highest gain in any scam business is the knowledge that it is a scam. It is invaluable and outweighs any of the past financial losses you have incurred in that scam business.

CHAPTER 9

SCAM INPUT

Several situations have been attributed to scams and scams have also greatly impacted our daily lives. Looking at certain past businesses and current ones, it may be surprising to notice a kind of resemblance that exist between genuine businesses and scam businesses, making them difficult to differentiate.

Scam has changed the world and is gradually eroding trust. The world, as a global village, is and will always be a wonderful development that scams will threaten.

A man in Japan can now comfortably do business with another man in Atlanta without ever seeing each other. Payments, agreements and all that will be involved in the business can be concluded without their sitting face to face. The facility needed to make such business possible has been developed by mankind, but scam is the only thing that will create doubt in such a business transaction.

It might seem embarrassing, dishonorable or odd to suspect another gentleman or lady of being a scammer but it has become the right thing to do or you might get scammed.

I cannot remember how many times I recounted cash withdrawals in banks. I just followed the bank cashier's count, collected my money and left. Do you know that the very first day I recounted, I was short of 5 bills out of 200 bills. Can you believe that? I was so disappointed. Since then I always recount my bank withdrawals after the cashier's count. I can say that, in twenty recounts there was shortage in three of them.

This is the world we live in now and nothing to be ashamed of. Recount your money, check your purchases, recalculate your change, make sure of your deliveries, etc. Do not assume. On no condition should you assume it is okay without witnessing the okay yourself. (See Chapter 29—*Transaction Vigilance*)

Before any business transaction takes place, politely tell your business partner no matter whom, that you will check the whole thing out first before proceeding. There is nothing indecent, there is nothing insulting in doing so; you are just taking precautions so that the business will be fine from day one. In peculiar cases where scammers may be using your friend, your business partner or your relation without their knowledge, you might also be rescuing them, by checking out the whole thing before proceeding. Always check out the whole thing before proceeding, do not allow anyone to hustle you for any reason.

One of the main causes of concern for a scammer is delay. Delays spoil scams and scams spoil with delays. The scammer likes to get the prospective victim committed as fast as possible because, when you are committed, your reasoning starts wavering.

Scams are becoming real businesses; I mean people are opening companies for the sole purpose of scamming unsuspecting clients. This is getting very common and the internet is facilitating such transactions. People are taking the time to design complete bank websites for the purpose of perpetrating scams and identity thefts. Governments do not scam people but the human beings who work in government can be scammers.

A top director in a country's national bank was accused of using his office to scam a foreigner; the director denied the allegation, claiming he was not in the country then. Evidence showed that he was actually away, attending a foreign seminar in Hamburg when the scam occurred.

If it was his office or not, I cannot categorically say, and I do not know if his colleagues in the office were involved or not, but the fact is that the description offered by the scam victim during cross examination in court resembled his office.

These kinds of things are possible. They are possible because everyone wants money; they might not know the quantity exactly but they want easy money.

'$10,000 to use your office for 5 minutes' is a wonderful offer that might be difficult to reject.

'$10,000 to use your director's office for 5 minutes' is a more wonderful offer, which might be more difficult to reject.

Importing anything now without seeing the imported goods physically before they are containerized is risky. For instance, these days you buy a refrigerator brand only to discover that its compressor is of another brand. There is also no shame in telling the seller that you would like to see the compressor in the refrigerator you are buying and the maker's name. On the other hand, tell the seller to give you a comprehensive warranty.

Personally, I cannot trust a bank online without physically visiting their office. This is the world in which we live today. So many things have become so confusing that everything needs to be double-checked to ensure their validity.

A local adage says;

'Even as their mother, I can only vouch for my baby in my womb, and never for the child I am carrying on my back'.

When globalization and the latest technologies fastened business processes, everyone was happy. Many businesses adopted them and ended up losing a lot of money to scammers. It became clear that since scams took full advantage of these technologies, businesses are starting to go back to the old practices. It might be slower but more verifiable. It is now common for online financial businesses to request proper identification papers to open accounts, and they will send documentation to the submitted address to verify its existence. The same day business conclusions are on the decrease as businesses now need time to check every customer's claim thoroughly in order to build a base of trusted customers.

Anything is possible. Many are involved in businesses they do not know are scams, many will be used purposely to lure others into scams and many more will be used unknowingly to lure yet others into scams. Scam has brought so much misery, and to avoid scams, every business should be subject to checks and verifications—no excuses and no trust. No matter who is involved and the level of the business. You might not only be saving yourself but a whole lot of others.

PART 2

THE SCAM BUSINESS PROCESSES.

Every business has a process, be it contract, trading, import, export, banking, transport, retail, domestic or international, etc. All transactions called "business" transactions have a process. It starts somewhere and concludes somewhere for business to have been carried out.

Business processes vary from place to place but there are still constants. A good example of a business process is collecting a payment receipt after buying a plasma TV from an electronic shop.

To understand a business is to know the basic processes that occur in such a business. Modifying these basic processes to maximize profit is secondary to the primary concern, which is to know the business processes. All scams businesses have business processes.

CHAPTER 10

SCAM BUSINESS INTRODUCTION AND PRESENTATION MEDIUMS

Presenting the scam proposal (business-looking proposal) to an unsuspecting target is a major process in scam business that must be well understood in avoiding scams. There are different means used by scammers in communicating their fictitiously beneficial business proposals to their unsuspecting victims. Almost all communication mediums are used by scammers, the main objective being to ensure that the intended target receives the scam proposal for consideration.

Most people have preferences in communication mediums and attach importance likewise. Some prefer postal mail, while others prefer emails or telephone calls, etc. These variations offer the possibility for a particular scam to be presented in several ways, using different mediums. Likewise, these various means of presentation impact differently to different people depending on their communication preferences, and is one reason that keeps producing scam victims. The storyline of each scam proposal can differ but the main objective remains the same—luring the target into parting with his or her money or personal details.

Without forgetting the usual contents of scam proposals; something to gain and a great opportunity (offer and sale of confidence), let us look at some mediums scammers use to present scam proposals to their eventual victims.

A: POSTAL MAIL:

This is receiving scam proposals through normal mail delivery system or courier services. This introductory method is very effective but slow for scammers who prefer other faster means of delivery. If the scam proposal is well constructed and sent by postal mail, it can create some level of trust. The receiver might believe he or she should take the proposer seriously. Most people treasure postal mail and believe the majority of correspondences they get through it. This trust in postal mail also comes from the fact that the majority of your genuine correspondences comes through the mail. Bills, checks, postcards, personal letters, insurance papers, court papers, credit cards, debit cards, mortgage papers etc., are received via postal mail. Identity theft scams are very common in postal mail. Your bank information can be stolen through postal mail. In certain cases of postal mail thefts, the correspondence is only photocopied while the original is still sent to the addressee. This will not arouse suspicion on the part of the addressee, while the scammer or fraudster perfects his or her next move based on the photocopied information. Another way scammers send out scam letters is just to assign any name to the mail and send it. Some wrongly addressed letters are adjusted by the post office service, so greedy receivers of such letter might think that their blessings are on the way having intercepted another's secret. They never realize that their sheer greed was the proposer's target

B: TELEPHONE/FAX:

Scammers also present scam proposals to their targets via the telephone or fax. Telephone includes landlines, cell phones and mobile phones SMS (text Messages). There are calls from unknown persons making wonderful investment proposals to you. Also calls from presumed old friends asking you to assist them in one thing or the other. Lottery and competition scams are conveyed via phone calls, notifying you that you have won a lottery draw. Recipients rarely ask when they entered the lottery they have won! The scammers are now getting smarter by claiming your email address was used for the lottery draw, which sounds more convincing and creates less suspicion regarding when you entered the lottery you won.

Scam proposals via telephone calls are very effective in quickly committing the scam target. People easily commit themselves by word of mouth than in writing. On the phone you can easily say "count me in". Once these words are pronounced, the scammer will move for an early commitment. It is easier to give your credit card or debit card details during an alluring phone call proposal, which the criminals will charge immediately.

I once got a call from a very polite lady based in the UK; she explained how I will appear in the world "who's who" publication and how this will be for a lifetime. She kept trying to persuade me

to subscribe immediately. The pressure she applied—gently mind you—was hard, so I gave her my card details for the $750 payment, mixing up the card numbers purposely. We were still on the same discussion when she informed me that the card details did not go through and asking me if I had another card. I told her I had no other card and will check the problem with my bankers. She started laughing and hung up.

You will notice that most product marketers prefer to call you on the phone than send emails. Telephone discussions provide an easier way to make someone invest or commit to something faster than through writing. A scammer who is very sure of his or her scam proposal, will prefer to call the scam target rather than writing.

Many scam targets think because they spoke with real persons on the phone makes the deal genuine. Some assume that scammers are people who hide all the time. No! Scammers always act with boldness. A scammer can call you on the phone and still meet you physically for further business talk. It has not yet become a crime to call someone or meet someone physically to transact a business; the premise being that the scam target can refuse the proposal at any time.

It is also important to know that in most telephone calls, it is difficult to check the person or his proposal out or hold anyone liable. There are so many telephone services, fax services, call forwarding services, switchbox services, fax to email—email to fax services. To worsen matters, the majority of these services some companies provide are free. The companies offering these free services somehow believe that after giving a user free service, the users will then make real purchases or subscribe. Some users do and some do not but it creates ample room for anyone to get any telephone numbers free as often as they want or need one. Without mentioning any names, there are so many websites and firms that offer free telephone and fax forwarding services. Just search 'free telephone and fax forwarding services' and you will be surprised how many firms do this all over the world. Some even offer free office services with office switchboards and secretaries. You can be anywhere in the world and claim you are in London or New York. The roaming services of most mobile phone companies have also aided telephone scams; since you can now be in one place and claim you are in another very easily. Less than 10% of people approached via telephone for an investment venture eventually check out the identity of the callers. How many people can take the time to check the caller's identity with the Better Business Bureau or consumer agencies, or even check the local phone book references? How many people are aware that you can still obtain caller IDs even when hidden?

Scammers on the phone know their victims can dispute transactions when they pay with credit cards. They are also aware that less than 20% of people scammed via their credit cards eventually dispute such transactions. Many scam victims see card charge disputes as a waste of time and simply change their cards. Out of every 100 phone scams via credit cards, the scammers are sure to withhold 50-60 no matter how notorious the scams were; because, many people do not understand these things. At worst the scammer can provide inferior service to what the credit card paid for. Another popular scam on the phone is the credit repair, I wonder how a credit report can be repaired if the information is correct. Information that can be repaired is information that is incorrect and has been proved to be so. This makes me wonder what the repair will be unless the intended repair is to forge the real report.

Scammers on the telephone are always in a hurry, they hardly give their scam target time, and they answer questions as soon as they are asked. The phone scam proposer prefers to know how soon the scam target will commit and the exact time, as if he or she couldn't "wait a second". It is normal for telephone scammers to give their prospective victim an extraordinary discount to make it easier to obtain immediate cooperation (offer/sale of confidence).

Phone scams are unlike written proposals where there is time for digestion, comparison and expert opinion consultations. Most scammers proposing on the phone will not send written proposals even when their targets request written proposals; they will give one reason or another and tell their scam targets to ask further questions as they wish. They know questions that scam targets and victims ask can easily betray their thoughts as they speak on the phone.

C: INTERNET:

The internet is one of the greatest inventions of the 20th century. More than 60% of scams are currently operating on the internet. The majority of scam proposals are sent to targets through the internet medium and the majority of people come across scam proposals on the internet. The internet has simplified practically everything, including business transactions. It has made New York search minutes away from Melbourne, it has made London search minutes away from Bangkok. The internet can inform anyone on anything. It can inform a layman on a doctor's procedure, specimens of important legal and government documents are on the internet, there are even websites that can help you draft any legal document on the internet. You can act a lawyer, engineer or any other profession using information on the internet. Internet searches can disclose peoples' emails and telephone information. The internet can even display your physical picture and your full biography without your permission. Internet search experts can find out most things they seek. More search engines are being developed daily. The internet has grossly favored both the genuine person and the scammer or con artist. Generally, the internet is very attractive to most people as it has made all types of business transactions cheaper by reducing business costs. Most businesses prefer the internet for their transactions. The scammers and the con artists would have been spending millions distributing their numerous proposals if not for the internet. A scammer can now easily reach a million people by the click of a 'send' button. The email is internet based and a wonderful development in dispersing business proposals. Email sends and receives messages by reaching anyone anywhere in seconds. There are websites gathering email addresses. There are email addresses on sale. There are software programs that can extract email addresses from websites. The majority of internet users believe above 80% of whatever they discover on the internet. Most people will check for any answer only on the internet. The internet has the latest dictionaries and can meaningfully, translate any major language into another in mere seconds. The internet has assisted scammers in perfecting frauds and scams generally.

A situation where a lady asked who is the finance minister of her country, consults the internet immediately will only leave the fate of those awaiting her answer, as to when the resulting information was fed into the internet. This is the real situation these days; people hardly listen to the radio or TV news but search the internet for the latest news items. Most people do not know how to search for certain information again, except on the internet. They do not know about government information help desks, they simply consult the internet and believe whatever they come across. There are professional hackers for hire; do not be surprised to learn that some scammers employ internet hackers full-time. There are fake mailer websites on the internet that can impersonate genuine email addresses of genuine persons, organizations and government agencies. There are phishing links, phishing websites, pharming sites, password extractors, data extractors. Most things which scam targets, prospective scam victims and scam victims think are not possible are very possible on the internet.

There are sites you will visit on the internet that will steal your password and email addresses. Directions to these sites can come in different forms like a mail to your home address or a telephone call from your account officer. The information will advise you to change your login details for security upgrade. Your login details will be stolen the moment you open these sites and fill in your data for any upgrade as directed. Recently, these scammers use money payment slips you can only see by logging in with your email address and password. Many victims fall for this as it involves a money payment slip. Victims hardly ask themselves, if they were expecting any payment from anyone, even if they were, why do you have to login with your details in order for you to see your payment receipt.

The internet has aided good and bad. People use the internet to do things that astonish everyone. Criminals and evil doers can comfortably take responsibilities for heinous crimes punishable by death on their internet websites.

The internet has reduced the cost of doing business making it attractive to all.

A Japanese businessman in Tokyo might be skeptical about traveling to Liberia to sign business documents due to cost, security or other reasons. The internet simplifies this for him; by requesting that the documents be sent to him via email attachments, which he will peruse, print, sign and send back. The Japanese man will also forget that he has missed the opportunity to physically vet the business, which a one-on-one meeting with his Liberian business partners could have offered him. It is possible that those Liberian government officials he is dealing with are young men in their early twenties and not government officials. The same Japanese man might also send money to his Liberian partners to hire an attorney to sign the documents on his behalf, having read the well written documents sent to him by email. So, the Japanese man could have lost the opportunity to physically vet the business twice, plus his money in attorney fees, all because he received an email via the internet.

There is need for business people to realize that certain businesses require physical meetings or the business should not be carried out. If you assess a business venture and cannot be physically present, you might as well forget about the business entirely. This attitude acts as a guide most times and is very effective in protecting you against any potential scams.

Some local adages say;

'Face fear face'.

'What I will do to that lion' is normally in its absence.

It can be expensive, complex and difficult to physically imitate certain scam stages. It is not easy to imitate President Mugabe's son in Harare. It could have been very difficult for the young Liberians mentioned above, to physically convince the Japanese businessman that he was a guest of the honorable Minister of mines in Liberia if the Japanese businessman had gone to Liberia. The internet simply hastened his conviction of the business process having seen the whole business documents via email.

Internet is a perfect medium in presenting scams. It also has the ability to store and retain well planned scam proposals as websites for anyone who comes across it to consider. Emails reach recipients in seconds at virtually no cost. You can set email auto-responders to reply any email with whatever you desire. The majority of investment scams have websites on the internet. Fake banks have websites on the internet. There is so much misinformation and false materials already posted on the internet by fraudsters that even a genuine search can lead to them. Scammers also use internet adverts to generate traffic to their scam sites. Many internet pop-ups will lead surfers to scam sites. The internet has websites, software and programs with the ability to reproduce documents, correct grammar, spelling, etc., making things appear as the originals.

High Yield Investment Programs (HYIPs) scams, investment scams, online auction scams, online goods purchase and service scams, money transfer scams, identity thefts, bank frauds, lottery winning scams, porno service scams, bequest scams, charity donation scams, holiday or vacation scams, pyramid scheme scams, etc. are all on the internet with beautiful interactive websites. You come across these scam websites and you are not properly informed, you are in, and the scam has started.

Most people believe any company with a website is genuine and existing. Most people cannot check the location of another internet user. They cannot do an ISP location check. Even in some cases, where they know how to check the sender's ISP, people simply disregard it. To worsen matters; there are software programs that can change your ISP location. This means that you can be anywhere and claim to be elsewhere. Many scam HYIPs are now on the internet and make use of only particular online payment solutions, I am sure is also set-up by them. Scam has become well organized with the internet.

Do not judge anyone or any business by their internet presentation; unbelievable things can be done on the internet.

The internet and businesses emanating from it have shown their uniqueness; the internet can advertise, support, contradict, encourage, and discourage any business.

The main point remains that everyone must have another means to use and obtain accurate information on things you surf on the internet. Do not rely solely on the internet. There are other verifying processes of authenticating internet information still available. Checking out a company physically will always be better than checking their registration certificate posted on their website. We looked at this in Chapter 8—*Understanding Gains and Losses*. Presently on the internet, you can fully register a new company today without having a physical address. There are even secretarial agencies that can run this newly registered online company for you, acting company secretary, answering call and messages like a functional firm.

Mrs. Agnes can prepare a document that New York is in India and post on the internet, likewise, Mr. Bern can prepare another document claiming that New York is in Europe. An internet search on New York can show the two documents with their respective information. Both are wrong and you will need to know exactly how to search information correctly in order to get the correct answer that New York is in the United States.

How many people who search the internet frequently know how to 'search'? Scammers can post a story on the internet and start scamming people based on that story. This is common.

Email and its rapidity is a great advantage to scammers. Bear in mind that scams can be very spontaneous. Scammers use email extractors to get people's email address and contact information. At times scammers buy this information or come across it mysteriously, in a manner which is difficult to understand.

When I visited the USA, I opened an account online with eBay. The next day while socializing with my friends, one Mr. Stewart called me. He said that he could assist me in making money selling several products online. He offered to design a website for me that would automatically direct online buyers who visit the website to the manufacturer's websites and keep the commissions for me. The cost would be $5,000 and the site would be fully automated so I didn't need to bother; I had heard of such business so I was comfortable. When I asked him how he knew me, he said I was referred to him by eBay. Everything coincided with my online registration on eBay the previous day. I told him that I did not have any credit cards or debit card to make any deposit for him to start. He said their company had agents nationwide and that one of their agents in my location could be with me in the shortest possible time so that I could take advantage of the ongoing discount. Later on, the same day, I physically met with Mr. Alan, his local agent, and gave him the $1,000 deposit to proceed with the website design. To date I never heard from Mr. Stewart or Mr. Alan again. Both their number are permanently connected to an answering machine, as a matter of fact.

What destroyed any suspicion I might have had previously was the physical meeting we had. Later on I found out that Mr. Stewart was not referred by eBay. Mr. Stewart was a sure scammer who must have gotten my phone number through my friends or some disgruntled company worker somewhere, or through other mysterious means. One thing was sure; he knew I opened an eBay account online. That was confusing and when I inquired from eBay; they knew no such Mr. Stewart and neither operated that way. These mysteries are common in scams. In Chapter 7—*The Cyberspace* we have already described how scammers can get your private data. I cannot be definite how they got mine but they played the whole scam very well. Mr. Alan was a Caucasian man, assertive in his manner, and really talented. Imagine the effect he would have on an African man visiting North America for the first time.

His demonstrations and explanations were very good and he was very convincing. His explanation for the automatic website design plan was superb; I only had to make the $1,000 deposit.

Scams on the internet are complex; surfing can lead to many other scams that most scam target are not aware of. It is common in internet scams, to start one thing that will end as another thing or another scam. ***Be careful of what you meet on the internet for the internet is a perfect scam stage and the most active scam stage.***

D: PHYSICAL CONTACT:

This is the person to person meeting and personal presentation of scam proposal. The introducer might be doing this knowingly or unknowingly. Scam proposals can be physically presented to you by someone you know very well. A relation or a good friend can meet you and convince you to invest in a scam business. In most cases, the introducer or presenter does this unknowingly, but there are several cases where the presenter is fully aware of what will happen to you ultimately and decides to go ahead for a share in the scam profit. Some physical scam proposal presenters are ***professional scammers themselves***, and your relation or friend can be one unknown to you. They fully understand your personality and what your reaction will be should the scam go on, or if it failed. Another group of introducers are mere acquaintances and you see them as ***prospective business contacts*** to maintain. Then lastly, the '***first contact***' introducers; they are people you rarely know nothing about, just met them someplace with or without much reflection. All these introducers are very effective because of some element of trust they exhibit in the physical discussions, on which they capitalize.

Scam proposals, when presented physically, have a way of disarming your instincts, and consoles scam targets with the idea that there is someone to hold responsible should anything go wrong. Many scam targets who became prospective scam victims and eventually scam victims, relied solely on their physical assessment abilities during such encounters with scam proposal presenters, which misled them.

Physically presented scam proposals are very effective. Many people think that physically presenting scam proposal is solely about the scammer meeting you and suggesting that you participate in a scam business. No! It can involve that and much more. Scam proposals can be presented physically in different ways such as you would never recognize them as scam proposals. Physically presented scams are the most effective because they have the ability to disarm even the most informed person on scams. Let us see this scenario;

Your cousin unknowingly invested $50 in a scam HYIP scheme. Two days later as the HYIP advertised, he now had $60 (20% profit). Four days later he had $72. Good business. Your cousin tried to withdraw his initial $50 investment and it went through successfully. He told his wife, who also invested $50 and got the same $72 after 4 days. Meanwhile your cousin is also paid a 20% commission for introducing his wife who invested $50. Withdrawals are all going well, and referral commissions are being paid. If you are financially better off than your cousin, with what vigor and seriousness do you think he will introduce this HYIP to you? He will even make you feel that your refusal to invest in such a money yielding venture is sheer wickedness toward him since he would not get his 20% commission. He might convince you to put in $2,000 or more. Your $2,000 becomes the target and then the same money yielding HYIP website that has been paying others will ultimately shut down without a trace.

The above is a good example of the possible sequence in a physically presented scam. Your cousin and his wife have not been scammed but you have. Scammers prepare their scam schemes very well, both in presentation and management. These scammers monitor their investors and also monitor who their investors introduce by promising commissions for introducing others. For the seasoned scammer, everything is under watch and analysis. They make their investors their marketers by promising referral commissions.

Your best marketer for your business is your past customer.

The purpose of the entire referral commission offer is to make past customers their marketers, which is more effective than the company's direct marketing. Unfortunately, this is also applicable to scam schemes. The main reason behind this is that;

Past customers market mainly by physical contact presentation.

A closer observation will show that most investors on the above HYIP scam will be busy introducing the HYIP to friends and relations while the HYIP scammer waits for the target victim—the big investor. It is also possible you could not have invested more than $100 based on what you have heard previously about such HYIP scams, but your cousin was so convincing and very persuasive. It was a trust scam introduced physically. You might have previously heard all the news and all the information to avoid such HYIP scams, but when it is presented physically with trust, it can disarm you. The above HYIP might have never convinced you to invest with all their advertisement and marketing skills, or your cousin might never have convinced you either if he had written to you, but by physically meeting you, the whole thing looked different. Only few people can still detect such physically presented scam proposals and resist them.

Your cousin has simply convinced you to invest in a scam business unknowingly. Your cousin's motivation was for you to make more money and in that process he would make money too, through his referral commissions and the further investments he might make. Your $2,000 loss has covered the HYIP scammer's initial profit payments to your cousin and his wife with enough net profit for the scammer.

If on the other hand, your cousin did not contact you, the HYIP scammers above, after some time could have deduced, through their monitors that your cousin's ability to bring in more capable clients for referral commission is very slim; they simply would have scammed your cousin directly. Fortunately for your cousin, he showed his marketing abilities by recruiting first his wife within days, then you.

Scam proposals can also be presented physically by persons you know or trust who are not related to you. They can be part of your social or work settings. The presentation can also be done knowingly and unknowingly. Scams can appear as a very good business venture introduced to you by a person working for you or a neighbor, but the business requirement makes the person working for you an unsuitable partner in the venture. Scam can also be the business venture of your superiors, yet, and because of their position, travel constraints, language or other inability, you are sent to represent him or her. Knowingly or unknowingly you can simply facilitate and assist the scamming of your superior, you being the one having physical contact with the scam target. **During the staged signing of the final release order of a certain transaction Mr. Yen Kim (Korean man) had in Accra, Ghana, his** interpreter Mr. Noda—also from Korea—purposely changed Mr. Yen Kim's receiving account details to his own personal account as the ultimate beneficiary. Mr. Yen Kim could not understand a word of English, let alone understand the written word, so he signed the paperwork, and they left. In order for Mr. Noda to conceal his actions, he ensured all correspondences about the business, mails, and calls went through him and in that process he lost close to $700,000 while pursuing the business. Later on, when Mr. Noda was out financially, he started convincing Mr. Yen Kim to pay the scammers. He kept reassuring Mr. Yen Kim that all was okay and that the business was genuine. Mr. Yen Kim lost another $1,500,000 in addition to Mr. Noda's $700,000.

Mr. Yen Kim in this case, may or may not have paid the scammers, he could have exhibited some caution as a seasoned business man whether he spoke English or not. But, the physical contact he has with dishonest Mr. Noda had perfected this scam. Even if Mr. Noda had in mind to distribute gains equally afterwards, his actions of changing the account had created room for the scammers.

A successful scam might be in progress, when there is someone maintaining physical contact with the scam target and encouraging the target knowingly or unknowingly.

Mr. Noda was acting unknowingly in this case. It was when he ran out of money that he started bringing in Mr. Yen Kim into the scam payments. By the time Mr. Noda started involving Mr. Yen Kim in the payments, he must have become obsessed with the success of the business and his priority then would have been mere success, having spent so much. He did not care whose account the money now entered or was changed. His belief would be that no matter what, he would let the business run its course and would settle the matter with Mr. Yen Kim later. Unfortunately, it was too late because the business was a scam from day one. Mr. Noda might have been trying to imitate Mr. Yen Kim's success from the outset; he might have seen such transactions as the key to Mr. Yen Kim's past great successes in Seoul. The main fact here is that Mr. Noda garnished the scam being in direct physical contact with Mr. Yen Kim.

One must properly screen his or her workers before they lead you to a scam. Also, inform your relations and workers properly. Let them have an idea of your income. When you are secretive you create the impression that you do 'wonderful things' to make money and that might lead them into presenting scam proposals to you, knowingly and unknowingly. The most reliable way to scam anyone is to send someone he or she knows physically and trusts. If you can trust your worker with your security, then you also trust his words too.

A disgruntled gateman informed his master of twenty years that his friend who visited him eight months ago left a big box with him. He claimed that all efforts to reach his friend were fruitless and that he did not know the contents of the box. He was afraid and decided to let his master and mentor know the situation before problems would arise (a good and worthy gateman!). His master wanted to see the box and when he did, he opened it. The box was filled with black paper cut to the size of US Dollars bills money with instructions on how to clean it. They followed the instruction and cleaned some of the black papers with the sample cleaning chemical also included in the box as instructed. The black papers were real US dollar bills and the master entered the scam stage. They now needed more chemical to clean the rest of the black papers and the master was now very interested. The master later on spent close to $650,000 trying to clean the rest of the money that amounted to about $17,000,000 in cash.

The gateman in this case was well aware of the trunk's content and knew how the scam would work. Moreover, he was sure of the master's greed, knowing very well that his master would fall for the scam. Locating how to buy more chemicals to clean the black money, communications, etc., were all previously arranged. Waiting for the master to buy the story was the only remaining part of the scam scheme. The main attribute to this scam was the physical contact based on trust. This same scam might have failed if it was presented by email or mail, but when presented physically, it did not. The master might be aware of such 'wash money scams' but might be unable to relate those with this physical presentation.

If you read more scam stories, you will notice that in most cases—seven out of ten—the scams are always successful when the victims were met in person. Even paying scam victims paid more after a physical meeting.

Summarily, Scams can also be introduced using a combination of these mediums. Huge scams that lasted long involved the use of almost all these communication mediums or a combination of two or more of these communication mediums.

CHAPTER 11

DIFFERENT FORMS OF SCAMS

Scams being dishonest plans for making money, there are different kinds of plans adopted by scammers in unknown transactions. Scammers use the communication mediums discussed in the last chapter to present their proposals to their targets with the primary objective of extracting money, obtaining information or making a profit from these targets.

A particular scam can appear in a different situation as a different scam. Likewise, a particular scam proposal can have different meanings to different recipients. For instance, a scam proposal received by an individual might have another meaning when received by a business entity. A lawyer can interpret a scam proposal differently from a doctor. It is also important to note that a scam can begin as one type and end as another type of scam. For instance, a scammer extorting money from a date in a dating or romance scam can still lure that date into a money transfer scam set by the same scammer. It is common for a scammer to present different forms of scams in a relationship with a scam target (prospective scam victim), as long as the primary objective of extracting money, obtaining information or making a profit from the victim is being accomplished. In major scam cases where scam victims were heavily scammed, many forms of scams were in play.

Scammers, in order to appear genuine, will tailor their scams to suit their targets' available information as much as possible. Priorities vary; scam targets, prospective scam victims and scam victims display various approaches to issues and matters. These varied attitudes towards matters incline the scammers to tailor their scams to suit the available information on their targets. For instance, an investment scam proposal will naturally interest a scam target seeking a profitable investment haven rather than a dating scam proposal.

There will be repetitions as we discuss the different types and forms of scams, these repetitions are simply specific to the matters under consideration.

There are different forms of scams presently going on worldwide and new scams are being developed daily, due to the uniqueness of individuals and transactions possible. Scams can be classified into different forms, from the view point of the scam target they are designed for.

Listed below are the major groups most scams can be classified into;

1. INVESTMENT SCAMS:

They are scam schemes cleverly designed to trick scam targets out of their money by promising very high returns on investments. They can be very sophisticated and the scammer puts a lot of pressure in persuading scam targets to invest. Investments scams are one of the oldest scams. They have been around even before the invention of the telephone and internet. Investment scammers always claim you are privileged to be aware of the investment. The investment is normally risk-free but you are approached by someone out of the blue. Investment scam schemes are marketed mainly by telephone, physical contact and the internet, and because many people trust their postal mail, investment scams are very effective when presented via postal mail.

Some investment scams are seen as:-

Cold call scams: These are unsolicited phone calls from unknown persons proposing high-returns on high-risk investments, often in overseas markets. The callers sound professional and will normally prefer an immediate investment no matter the investment amount.

Share promotion & 'hot tips' scams: They are email messages or strange phone calls that urge you to buy shares in a thinly-traded company. Normally, the scammer will give out information about the shares that look privileged and why it should be taken advantage of immediately. Possibly, the share company has made great progress that will become public in the future, etc. The scammers' purpose might be to push sales on a particular share from which they will benefit or wait until their victims invest before selling their own dead stock at a profit.

Investment seminars and real estate scams: Common these days are the forex trading seminars. Scammers profit through attendance fees and by selling properties and investments at inflated prices. The scammer advantage here is the reality that surrounds seminar attendance (a physical contact medium) and the excellent demonstrations at these seminars. They are high-pressure sales in high-risk investment strategies.

Sports investment scams: Expensive software packages that promise to predict the results of sporting events or share market movements. Some forex trading robots that guarantee certain daily trading profits are good examples of these scams. When they fail to work as promised, refunds are hard to come by.

Superannuation scams: You are offered early access to your superannuation ('early release'), often through a self-managed super fund. The scammers take a large part of your super for themselves, and put you at risk for accessing your super in an illegal way.

Ponzi schemes: These are advanced investment scams set up by many suspicious financial institutions purportedly paying huge profits on investments or huge interests on deposits. These financial institutions claim to be local investment firms in their vicinities or community banks. In these scams, the supposed profits or interests are simply paid to early investors from money actually invested or deposited by later investors. Ponzi scams are very effective when operating in small localities and developing towns. It is common for perpetrators of Ponzi schemes to be in remote localities where governmental influence is reduced. Ponzi scheme perpetrators are likely to use other business activities to shield the Ponzi schemes. Moreover, it has the trust of a physically introduced scam because later investors in the scheme can easily access past investors who are neighbors actually, making use of past customers as best marketers. Ponzi scheme is a very advanced scam that governments must detect and stop.

2. SMALL BUSINESS SCAMS:

They are scams specifically designed and targeting mainly small businesses. Small business scammers are often very successful because small business owners want to grow their businesses. These scams can appear as bills for advertising or directory listings in a local publication, magazine, etc. They can also appear as government workers soliciting one fee or the other on behalf of the government, such as advertising, sign post and sanitation fees. Small business scam proposals can be presented by telephone, postal mail, and internet but more effectively by physical contact. These scammers are sophisticated and very persuasive with all their convincing materials and documents in hand. Small business scammers are also quick to threaten punishment for non compliance, often employing bullying. Another common feature of these kinds of scams is that negotiations for lower charges are easily accepted by the small business scammers, unlike in real governmental applicable fees.

Some scams targeting small businesses are;

Directories and advertising charge scams: Small businesses can be misled into paying for a directory listing or other advertisements that may not exist or were not authorized. These scams are very common given the great number of small business owners who wish for their business to grow, particularly when offered advertisements to increase their sales.

Trademark publication scam: This scam involves a scammer sending an unsolicited letter or invoice for payment for a trademark listing to a small business. The scammer tries to give the impression that they are connected with the registration of trademarks authority or an overseas-based equivalent. They claim responsibility for the publication, and what the small business stands to gain by registering is blown out of proportion.

Fax back scams: Unsolicited faxes offer great deals on products, entry into competitions or huge discounts and fantastic deals. Scammers targeting small businesses usually offer directory entries, trade and business lists, and catalogues of goods and services. These offers require you to send a fax back to a premium rate number to accept. Without the knowledge that you are paying high faxing fees for accepting to fax back, the scammers make sure your fax takes several minutes to go through, which means you end up with high, and unnecessary phone bills.

Office supply scams: The office supply scam involves being charged for goods you never ordered or never received, or receiving goods that were not what you thought you agreed to buy. The scammer will call you pretending to be your regular supplier, telling you that the offer is 'special' or is 'available for a limited time'.

Domain name scams: In this scam, small businesses with domain names are sent unsolicited invoice or email for an internet domain name registration very similar to their own business domain name or a renewal notice for your actual domain name. The notice could be from a business that supplies domain names trying to trick you into signing up to their service or it could be from a scammer trying to take your renewal money or domain names protection money. This scam is often successful as many domain name owners hardly remember their domain renewal dates.

Investment scheme scams: This type of scam usually involves telemarketing campaigns specifically targeting small business owners. Peddled as tax-free opportunities, these are often sports betting schemes or betting software offers in disguise and are nothing more than gambling.

Overpayment scams: This sort of scam involves scammers making contact to purchase goods and services from a small business. They then send to the small business a payment by cheque or money order for far more than the agreed price. The scammer then asks you to refund the overpayment or to pay the scammer's 'freight company'. The scammer is hoping you will transfer the refund or pay for 'freight' before you discover that their cheque has bounced or that their money order is phony. It has also been modified with identity theft; where the scammer will over pay genuinely with another person's payment information and demand you refund the excess. You might end up in serious problems.

Advert fee scams: These scams involve persons pretending to be working for one government arm or authority and collecting advert fees, sign post advert fees, etc., from unsuspecting businesses. The scammers normally come during business hours when most developing businesses will not like their customers to witness such embarrassments. These scams are very common in developing countries where the payments of such fees are not properly automated.

3. IDENTITY THEFT SCAMS:

They are scams that involve stealing money or gaining other benefits by pretending to be someone else. Identity theft scams can occur by somebody else using your credit card to purchase goods or services. The scammer assumes to be you and can use the information in many financial dealings that you are not aware of. The scammer will conduct illegal businesses under your name and identity he or she has stolen. A determined scammer can also create elaborate and cunning plans to trick you into providing your personal details. It is important to note that most of our personal information is readily available; cards in our wallets, mail, social media, public records, etc., making it easy for a scammer to obtain. Identity theft happens easily and quickly.

Identity theft scams appear as;

Phishing scams. By sending an email that looks like it comes from your bank, financial institution or telecommunications provider. These emails are all about tricking you into handing over your personal and banking details to scammers. Most work by including special links in the email to take you to a combination of genuine and spoofed websites.

Phony fraud alerts scams: These scams are similar to phishing scams where scammers trick you into handing over your personal details. A common fraud alert involves the scammer pretending to be from your bank, informing you that your credit card or account has been cancelled because of suspicious criminal activities (various excuses are used). They will then trick you to provide account details to 'confirm' your identity. The fraud alert can be sent via email, mail or telephone call.

Bogus job opportunities are usually posted on job websites. The scammer may use or sell your personal information provided in the job application.

4. HEALTH SCAMS:

These are scams offering solutions or cures to people who have medical conditions. Naturally, most victims of this kind of scams are worried about their health, and their medical conditions are exploited by these scammers. The scammers' cures and solutions are nonexistent and the main objective is to extract funds from their scam targets. This kind of scam, apart from costing the scam victim money, can also cause serious damage to the victims' health.

Health Scams often appear as;

Fake online pharmacy scams: Fake online pharmacies offer drugs and medicines at very cheap prices or without a prescription. Many people seeking to secretly buy certain drugs end up with these scammers. They can cause you major health and money problems.

Miracle cures scams: Miracle cure scams prey on the sick or desperate by selling drugs or treatments that don't work or are even dangerous. These scams are all over the internet. This and that herbal cure, ancient cure, etc.

Weight loss scams: False claims are made to mislead you into buying 'revolutionary' pills, creams, diet advice or machines that will aid you in losing excess weight. Losing weight is one major propellant of this scam in developed nations where the scam thrives very well.

5. CHAIN LETTERS AND PYRAMID SCHEME SCAMS:

These two scams are very old scams normally introduced via postal mail or physical contact where they are very effective. They can be comfortably presented to you by a person you know very well. In most cases the people introducing you to them might not be fully aware of what is going on as they, themselves, are trying to make profit as promised by the scheme operators (scammers). Pyramid scheme and chain letters are related. People who become involved in these scams can only make money by scamming other people. It works like a chain reaction.

This kind of scam appears in two main ways;

Chain letter scams: They falsely promise financial or other benefits for a relatively small cost. The more letters you can distribute the bigger the reward you will get. Chain letters contain a list of names along with a simple instruction. You are usually requested to send money to the top person on the list. Then remove the top person from the list, lifting the second name to the top position and add your name to the bottom position. You will then be directed to send out the letters and make money since your name will keep climbing upwards on the list. At times, all payments made on a chain letter can be designed to benefit one person actually.

Pyramid schemes scams: Illegal schemes that always collapse when the supply of victims dries up, leaving nearly everyone involved much worse off. The main identity of a pyramid scheme scam is that earning money and gaining promotion within the scheme depends primarily on recruiting people to the scheme, and those new people recruiting more people into the scheme, and so on. Most people can detect pyramid schemes easily when presented physically but pyramid schemes can be very difficult to recognize as scams when seen as detailed websites on the internet where many will diligently adhere to the scheme's instructions. The explanation and design of these scam websites employing pyramid schemes will make it difficult to know they are what you know about pyramid schemes. Generally, pyramid schemes are unfair business practices because they are bound to be unfair to most participants. The reward for those at the top of the list comes from those below and eventually it will become impossible to recruit the number of people required to produce reward for everyone on the list.

6. BANKING AND ONLINE ACCOUNT SCAMS:

These scams aim to steal your bank account information and your money. They are top scams with suitable websites and educated scammers. Internet banking has aided this particular scam. The ways we pay for goods and services have been modified globally and unfortunately, scammers are taking advantage of new technologies to generate a number of potentially very costly scams. Banking and online scams intend to steal your information and defraud you. Often they look real and genuine.

Banking and online account scams are rampant, appearing mainly in these forms;

Card skimming: Card skimming is the illegal copying of information from the magnetic strip of a credit or ATM card. This can create a fake or 'cloned' card with your details on it.

Credit card scams: There are many types of scams that aim to steal your credit card details, either by taking the card itself or by tricking you into giving them the card's details by phone or email.

Bank withdrawal scams: In this kind of scam, the scammer will call your bank pretending to be you. The caller will claim to be the owner of your bank account, stranded somewhere without cheque book or withdrawal book, etc., and in urgent need of money from his or her bank account. Your bank might be sympathetic and demand certain requirements before allowing such withdrawals. The scammer will meet these demands and withdraw your funds easily. The scammer is normally equipped with your bank statement and other requirements. This particular scam is rampant for offshore saving accounts that the account owners do not operate regularly. Later, it is always very difficult for you to prove to your bank that you did not withdraw the money.

Phony fraud alerts: Scammers call pretending to be from your bank or financial institution and tell you that there is a problem with your account. They ask for your account details to protect your money, but then use these details to steal your money.

Phishing' scams: Requests for your account information. Phishing emails are fake emails usually pretending to be from banks or other financial institutions. They make up some reason for you to give your account details and then use these details to steal your money.

7. JOB AND EMPLOYMENT SCAMS:

Job adverts can be scams and job interviews are perfect stages for scam. These are scams targeted towards people looking for a new job or a change of job. These scams often promise a much better income than the applicant could normally expect, and, if possible, guarantee it for a minor fee compared to what you will get when you secure the job. These scams are getting popular and the scammers will claim to originate from high salary paying countries or that they work as reputable employment agencies. They are very effective, but one thing is common, there must be an advance payment request before you get the job or income earning opportunity. The scammer can also use these employment stages to lure the job seeker into other scams easily.

Job and employment scams appear mainly as;

Work from home scams: Employment opportunities that promise huge incomes with little work while in the comfort of your home. The scammer is usually asking you to recruit new victims. Home makers fall for the scam so easily and the funniest thing in this scam is that one payment to the scammer leads to another as you continue to chase this mysterious work from home income.

Guaranteed employment/income scams: Scammers 'guarantee' you a job or a certain level of income, tricking you into paying an up-front fee for a 'business plan', materials, website or recruiting more victims indirectly.

Business opportunity scams: These scams comprise a range of scams marketed as business opportunities. They promise success but usually only the promoter makes any money.

8. INTERNET SCAMS:

The internet is one of the greatest inventions of our time. It has aided almost everything preceding it, including deceit. Internet scams are specially designed to take advantage of the way the internet works. The internet is the safest territory for scammers because it can hide identity, make anyone's trade cheaper and increases the ability to reach more scam targets faster. A lot of internet scams take place without the victim even noticing. It is only when their credit card statement or phone bill arrives that the person realizes that they might have been scammed. How you access the internet can also make a difference. One just cannot be sure of anything with some internet based websites, businesses and business transactions.

Internet scams operate out of the internet and they appear mainly as

Auction & shopping scams: These scams have great, attractive websites. Online auctions can be rigged by scammers or used to target you for a scam outside of the auction site. You could end up with a dud product or nothing at all for your money after winning a fictitious auction. The perpetrators are even perfecting auction scams by using their own bidding units they have modified like currencies, you buy expensively. The auction scammer can also claim that a nonexistent auction product has been won by someone. You may need to verify that for yourself after all. This scam is becoming very popular and the scammers are making a lot of money every day.

HYIP Scams: (High Yield Investment Program scams). These are scams that promise huge returns on investments based solely on the internet. They have beautiful websites and go in details to explain how you will make huge returns in short term investments, ranging from days to weeks and years. The scammers will claim to be investing your money in forex trading or one mysterious huge income earning business only they know about, supported with income calculators and tables. These well designed websites are owned by professional scammers as they monitor your investments, monitor those you introduce and will disappear as soon as they are satisfied with investor's funds so far. The scammers are also very articulate in manipulating you with returns on your investments.

Domain name renewal scams: Scams that send you a fake renewal notice for your actual domain name or a misleading invoice for a domain name that is very similar to your own.

Spam (junk mail) offers: Spam emails, SMS or MMS usually offer free goods or 'prizes', very cheap products or promises of wealth. Responding to spam messages can result in problems for your computer and your bank account.

'Free' offers on the internet: Offers of 'free' website access, downloads, holidays, shares or product trials—but in the agreement you have to supply your credit card or other personal details. It is common for these scammers to advertise a free month trial which you can cancel at anytime. How many victims will remember to cancel such and many of these scammers will charge your credit card sometime later without your knowledge. They can even charge your credit card in another transaction altogether and wait for your dispute.

Modem jacking: Modem-jacking scams secretly change the phone number dial-up modems used to access the internet to an overseas or premium rate phone number. You could pay hundreds of dollars extra.

Spyware & Key-loggers: Spyware is a type of software that spies on what you do on your computer. Key-loggers record what keys you press on your keyboard. Scammers can use them to steal your online banking passwords or other personal information.

Click fraud: This scam targets advertisers mainly. It occurs when an individual or computer program fraudulently clicks on an online ad without any intention of learning more about the advertiser or making purchase, but just to make the advertiser pay a fee for each click. Your competition can employ this to weaken your business by increasing your marketing costs. It is getting very serious and most reputable firms have no idea of click frauds.

9.   MOBILE PHONE SCAMS:

Scams that come to you on your mobile can be difficult to recognize. Cell phone scams are very effective; out of ten scams sent to your phone, you are likely to read nine if not all for consideration. They might come from somebody who talks as if they know you; they might come through a 'missed call' from an unknown number that you redial. They are upfront about what they are promoting, but have hidden charges. You might be offered free or cheap ring tones, or the chance to win fantastic prizes. When you reply to these messages or calls, you may find yourself disappointed in the product or signed up to a service you don't want or cannot stop. These scammers make accepting their offers (scams) very deceptive; replying to ask further questions might be construed as acceptance without your knowledge. You could be left facing a huge phone bill or monthly deductions you cannot stop.

Some mobile phone scams are;

Ring tone scams: These scams are misleading offers for 'free' or cheap ring tones that end up being a subscription or premium rate service.

Missed calls & text messages: These scams are missed calls from unknown persons that can lead to premium rate charges. Mysterious text messages that can cost a lot of money if your reply to them.

SMS competition & trivia scams: In this kind of scam, you are encouraged to enter a competition or trivia contest over SMS for a great prize—but misled about your chances or how much it will cost to take part.

Unexpected 'prizes': Unexpected prizes that need you to send money to claim—you may never receive the prize or it may not be what you expected. The majorities of new cell phone users take these notifications (scams) seriously and respond to them regularly.

10. LOTTERY AND COMPETITION SCAMS:

Lottery and competition scams are delivered in many ways—in person, over the telephone, through the post or by email. The scammer in this kind of scam will tell you that you've won something substantial (such as a large sum of money or a great prize) and that all you have to do is process the release your winnings, which will finally involve your sending some money as fees. Rather than winning a prize, you could lose a lot of money. Lottery and competition scam can also develop to other scams like 'money transfer' and 'wash money' scams, as the scammer tries to pay the winnings to you.

Most people secretly desire to win something, so lottery and competition scams are very common these days and they can appear as;

Lottery and sweepstake scams: Fake lottery or sweepstakes 'winnings' to tempt you into sending money or your personal details which is required for processing of your winnings.

Unexpected 'prizes': Unexpected prizes that need you to send money to claim—you may never receive the prize or it may not be what you expected. The scammer will tell you that you have won a prize in a competition in which you are fully aware you did not participate. To confuse the scam target further; the scammer can claim that your email addresses was used for the drawing which sounds more believable.

11. PERSONALISED SCAMS:

Personalized scams occur when scammers gather your personal information and use it to specifically target you with a scam. The fact that the scammer knows something about you may make you think they are legitimate. These scams have become more common in recent years and have taken on a new dimension in the online environment. Scammers target both individuals and businesses in this manner, inducing their targets to believe that they have been specifically selected to receive an offer while in reality; they will make the same offer to hundreds of people. These scammers use the internet to gather people's personal information, for example through social networking websites. They approach their targets by phone, SMS, letter, email, fax, or through online networking, dating or chat services and blogs.

Scammers often trawl the internet for your personal details and have also been known to search your mailbox or recycling bin to get hold of discarded personal documents such as bank statements and bills. The types of details these scammers search for include your name, date of birth, photos, income, occupation, email addresses (personal and work), telephone numbers (home, work and mobile), physical address (home, work or postal address), bank account and credit card details, social networking account, other personal numbers, such as Tax File and Medicare numbers, upcoming or current travel/holiday plans, relatives' and friends' names and contact details. When the scammers get hold of any of these details, they use them to pose as a legitimate government representative, a company, or a person you know and trust to scam you. The possibility for you to believe these scammers are very high because of the information they already have on you.

Personalized scams appear mostly as;

Charity scams: These scams play on your generosity and involve a scammer posing as a genuine charity in order to fraudulently collect money from you. When a charity you have previously made donations to, contact you again by phone, the possibility that you might not verify the caller is very high.

Classifieds scams: Classifieds scams can target both buyers and sellers who use online and print classifieds.

Dating and romance scams: Dating and romance scams try to lower your defenses by appealing to your romantic or compassionate side. They play on emotional triggers to get you to provide money, gifts or personal details. The scammers here can also use the existing relationship to lure their victims into doing fraudulent activities that will benefit the scammers.

Door-to-door and home maintenance scams: Door-to-door scams involve promoting goods or services that are not delivered or are of a very poor quality. The scammer either sells the products directly to you or use marketers who might not be fully aware of what they are selling.

Old hard drive scams. Scams can also originate from information previously stored in a disposed computer and the scammer can capitalize on this information. Always erase your hard drive before parting with old computers and laptops. Simply deleting individual files is not enough to remove personal details, documents and passwords stored on the machine.

Grooming scams: Grooming is when the scammer is building a relationship based on trust with a target by making regular contacts. Groomers use this relationship to extract greater amounts of trust, sensitive information and money from their victims. The scammer will be quite honest during grooming, trying to establish that trust that will be needed later for the scamming. The scam is very effective as it takes advantage of trust. Many victims never know it was because of previous grooming that they were ultimately scammed.

'Pharming' scams: Pharming is when you are redirected to a fake version of a website which may look identical to the website you were trying to view. The scammer will use the fake site to gather your sensitive personal information which they may then use to commit identity fraud.

Psychic & clairvoyant scams: If you are contacted by a psychic or clairvoyant offering you mystical secrets to wealth, health and luck, be very wary. Do not be fooled by fantastic claims and promises, many are scams using scammers who have some knowledge of psychology and can "invade" your mind for monetary gains or force you to release your private details.

Social networking scams: Social networking websites allow you to create your own profile and to interact with your friends and other online users. Friendship invitations and acceptances in these social media sites are being misused by scammers. Scammers also use social networking sites to steal personal information and trick people out of their money.

Victim lists: Victim lists are directories of people who have previously responded to a scam offer or fallen victim to a scam. These lists are created by scammers and contain personal information and contact details. They sell like hot cakes because scammers can tailor new scam proposals for those listed. They are compiled for the purpose of approaching those listed with other scams. HYIP investors' list is also one of them, containing a list of persons who have previously invested in similar HYIPs.

Job vacancy scams: In this type of scam, the scammer will get your information from the job applications you have submitted elsewhere. With your personal information and your desire to secure the job, you are likely to believe and follow the scammer's directives when they contact you.

'Whaling' and 'spear phishing' scams: Whaling or spear phishing occurs when scammers personally target employees in order to steal confidential business information and money. Scammers send emails about fake business matters aiming to convince their victims to follow a link to a scam website and provide confidential and financial details.

12. MONEY TRANSFER SCAMS: (Advance Fee fraud).

These are scams where the scammer promises to transfer money to you. Transferring this money to the scam target normally has a process which might involve advance payments from the scam targets and prospective victims. These are major scams because they have processes that appear as in genuine businesses to unsuspecting victims. They come in different forms and can also originate from genuine business basis. Internet banking has made it easier to transfer money across the world in minutes. Unfortunately, this has also meant an increase in the number and types of scams that try to trick you into sending money to overseas scammers. The scammers here may promise huge rewards or what looks like an easy way to make money. The same scammers can trick people who are trying to buy or sell products over the internet.

Some scams promising to transfer money are described below;

Over-invoiced sum scams: This particular type of scam plays in both genuine and scam situations. It can originate from a genuine business where the scammer will ask that the target should inflate the cost of whatever business they have so that they can share the over-invoiced sum later on. Now, because your real money (genuine earning) is tied to this over-invoiced sum, you will be eager and dedicated to see that the whole payment comes through; this is normally a perfect way to lure traders into scams they might be previously aware of. These scams involve a lot of expenses and fees being paid for your funds to come through.

Inheritance scams: An inheritance scam is when a scammer contacts you out of the blue to tell you that you've been left, or are entitled to claim, a large inheritance from a distant relative or wealthy benefactor who has died overseas. The scammer can also use your last name as the last name of the deceased whose relation they need and have been searching for.

'Nigerian 419' scams: They are called Nigerian 419 scams because of the section of the Nigerian penal code that deals with fraud and the frequency of such scams proposals emanating from Nigeria. Money transfer scams proposals can be sent by mail, fax, and phone call but most commonly by email in the form of a letter. Apart from Nigeria, such letters now come from any place in the world that suits the scammer's story. These scam proposals explain that the writer needs to access a foreign bank account through which money transfer may be effected. The amount of money usually mentioned is in millions of hard currency. The scammer needs the scam target's cooperation and assistance as the beneficiary of these funds. Details of your bank account for receiving the money and other requirements might also be needed as designed by the scammer. In return you are offered a good percentage of the transferred money and an opportunity to share in the millions. Many of these scam proposal letters refer to known political events or major disasters, which is often how the writer came to have access to such funds. The proposal is allegedly written by a government official, a prince, a top officer from a company or a quasi government corporation. The scamming process of this scam can make it last for years as the victim is mentally and financially extorted.

Up-front payment scams: You are asked to send money upfront for a product or 'reward'. You will end up with something much less than you expected, or nothing at all.

Transferring money for someone else: If you agree to transfer money for someone you don't know, you let scammers use your bank account to 'launder' their dirty money. This puts you and your money in the firing line.

Cheque overpayment scams: You are sent a cheque for something you have sold or selling, but it is far more than the amount agreed. The scammer hopes you will refund the extra money before you notice that the cheque has bounced. The scammer can also make the check or money order for the purpose of anything that will seem logical for a refund and this scam easily generate from genuine business situations. These scammers are also known to steal credit cards and use in these overpayment scams.

ATM withdrawal scams. These are scams where the scammer sends a debit ATM card to the scam target which has a real balance but might require removal of certain clause before withdrawals can be done with the ATM card. The scammer can alter this arrangement as he or she wishes as long as the target who is with the ATM card believes in the card. These scams are seen in money transfer scams or in big money businesses.

'Wash money' scams. These are scams that involve the cleaning of purported cash currencies that are in the form of blacks or stamped notes. These scammers might claim their scam targets will be paid via cash payment. These scams are seen in money transfers scams or big money businesses. The cash involved is normally disguised to hide it from the authorities for later cleaning. To clean the required currencies will involve the target purchasing cleaning chemicals and cleaning powders. They are very effective scams as the target might be in custody of the coded cash currencies or made to believe that they are safe somewhere while the target pays charges and fees. The target having witnessed the coded currencies and conversions to real spendable cash will believe and do anything to realize the money.

13. 'COME AND BUY' SCAMS:

These are scams targeted towards overseas buyer of particular goods and services. They are designed to attract these buyers based on the good's availability and relatively cheaper prices locally. These scams involve sales of gold, diamonds, platinum, crude oil and ammunitions. The scammers make their targets believe that they have stocks of the goods supported by their locality. The scam can involve some exposure to serious risks. They also involve some advance payments, bank guarantees, Letters of credit, etc., which to your greatest surprise the scammer will use or discount these bank instruments.

Come and buy scams appear as;

Ghana Scams: These are scams that involve a victim losing money in trying to buy gold or diamonds at relatively cheaper prices. It is common for the target to be introduced to the scammer via a reliable middleman in a developed country who is the scammer's partner in trade. The middleman's role is to implant the trust that will persuade the target. Even when the trade goes bad you still cannot hold the middleman responsible because he or she has carefully excluded themselves during the business process.

Kidnap Scams: These are scam situations where an overseas buyer is kidnapped at the point of purchase and ransom money are extorted from relations for his or her release. The scammers will lure their victims into traveling to their territory where they will be kidnapped or forced to do other things under duress.

Bank instrument scams: These are scams where the victim, in a bid to ensure a genuine purchase, is lured into preparing authentic bank instruments in favor of the scammer's directives which are later used or discounted through the scammer's connections. The scammer can also use these bank instruments otherwise. The scammers are highly connected, educated and well enlightened. They work hand in hand with reputed international mafia networks and syndicates when using the bank instruments.

Scarcity Scams: These are scams designed to make a scam target purchase certain goods at exorbitant prices from a target seller who is normally an accomplice of the scammer. The scammer is quick in creating artificial scarcity of the goods by ordering a very large quantity or making an earlier deposit for the goods. The scam target will be stuck with the goods after purchasing from the scammer's designed sellers for resale to the unknown scammer. Scarcity scams are very effective in most occurrences, although they are often underrated in commerce.

CHAPTER 12

UNDERSTANDING SCAM PROPOSAL RESPONSES

A scam proposal entails the description of a scam business scheme to a target. Scam proposal can come in the form of a letter, phone call, fax, email, physical meeting or a website. The scammer naturally will expect a response of 'Yes' or 'No' from the scam target after presenting the scam business proposal. The response of a scam target to a scam proposal can be encouraging or discouraging to the scammer. Commonly, most people who receive scam proposals and many scam targets give responses to the scam proposals without knowing what information they might have released.

Scam targets that receive scam proposals and accept to go into business with the proposer become prospective scam victims and might eventually become scam victims after losing money to the scammer.

It is glaringly clear in most cases that the scammer does not know all details about the scam target. As a matter of fact, the scammer gets to know the target better, from his or her actions as a prospective victim. The scammer tries to decipher the target's innermost desires, watching carefully and digesting all the target's actions, responses, and questions, trying to deduce or to learn where the scam target's weakness lies in order to eventuate fraudulent financial gains. Apart from greed, which is common in all scam victims, the mental and psychological attitude of eventual scam victims can easily be detected in their responses to the scam proposals.

Mr. Johnson, after receiving the proposal, which he never knew was a scam, responded:

'Oh, my good friend, I received your letter a bit late because you sent it to my smaller company . . .'

This response shows that Mr. Johnson likes the proposal, will go into the business, has many companies and is a rich man. Mr. Johnson has released all these information in just one sentence. By calling the sender "my good friend" Mr. Johnson has already shown that he has no doubt about the sender's personality. This response will ginger up the scammer to prepare the scam scheme carefully, because Mr. Johnson has shown in a few words that he is very capable and willing to go into the business.

The proposal and response in would-be successful scam is always a reciprocal desire game. Both the proposer and the responder will initially try to show their integrity. The proposer (scammer) will introduce the proposal (what is false) with confidence; likewise the responder (prospective victim) will be proving his or her capability in handling the said business. Bearing in mind that most decision making are affected by comfort level, confidence, risk tolerance, pride, predilection, past experiences, emotions, imitation and mere instinct, you will understand why your communication content can easily betray you to others.

There are three major responses to scam proposals and all scam targets-prospective victims' responses fall into one of this major three types of scam proposal responses.

A. POSITIVE RESPONSE TO SCAM PROPOSALS

This is a simple response of 'Yes, we can proceed' when the scam target receives the scam proposal or comes across the scam scheme and is firmly interested to go into the business. The scam target in this response to the scam proposals must have assessed his or her capability, judged the gains and decides to go ahead to do the business like in any other genuine business. Mr. Johnson's response above is a positive response of high grade. The scam target's acceptance might have been well conceived or not, what matters is that the target has accepted to go ahead with the proposal and has indicated interest firmly. When you invest time in any scam business scheme is a positive response. It does not matter whether you paid the scammer eventually or not. In avoiding scams you must add up all expenses in a scam business as unworthy. Even the telephone expenses, internet expenses and other expenses you incurred are all losses because the business is a scam. The only expenses that should be regarded as worthy are those expenses that convinced you to stop doing a scam business. We have discussed this in better details in Chapter 8.—*Understanding Gains and Losses.*

B. INTERMEDIATE RESPONSE TO SCAM PROPOSALS

Any response, reply or reaction to a scam proposal asking for further clarity on the proposal or even saying "not interested" is an intermediate response. It is intermediate because it can still become a positive response. The majority of scam proposal responses fall into this group. It is in this kind of response that the scam target, who has now become a prospective victim, ends up getting better convinced to do the business. It is also in this kind of response that the prospective victim ends up exposing his or her personality to the scammer.

Mr. Wang in his response asked**, 'how do you know me?'**

Mr. Saleh in his response asked**, 'If you were in Oxford, which class and year?'**

Mrs. Benson in her response asked, **'is your HYIP fully registered?'**

Mrs. Gates after registering on the website said, **'I hope this investment is real.'**

Mrs. Rommel replied, **'I have heard so much about scams and kindly note that I will not spend a penny for anything whatsoever!'**

Mr. Jose replied, **'I do not do business with strangers, we need to meet.'**

Mr. Akunne in his response asked, **'Sorry, I am unable to assist you. Thanks.'**

Mr. Kwale responded, **'Go to hell with your business!'**

As a matter of fact, these are all intermediate responses. They are all intelligent, genuine questions and responses but they all have answers. Scammers can provide answers to the best of their individual abilities. Their answers might convince or not convince the proposed victim. The issue remains that with the prospective victim's response, there is still room for the scammer's maneuvering which is not necessary when avoiding scams.

Mr. Saleh, in his above response, even attached 5 pages of scam publications for the scammer, showing he was aware of scams. The scammer carefully answered only Saleh's questions on Oxford University, insisting he could not cheat or deceive Mr. Saleh. The Oxford old student explanation was so convincing that Mr. Saleh trusted his old unknown school mate, who could not be deceitful. Sorry, his presumed "old school mate" was a scammer and he lost about $200,000. Was the explanation regarding Oxford University class and year an answer to the five-page scam publication Mr. Saleh had? No!

Even responses clearly stating that the responder is not interested can still become positive responses, depending on the scammer's convincing powers and sophistication. Scam victims do not get scammed only because they are gullible; the scammer's maneuvering skills are to be taken in serious consideration too.

Completing the registration form in an online-based scam is also a positive response. Asking questions through the website's help centre is also a positive response. They are positive responses because you have considered something in the content of the proposals that looked realistic or partially realistic for you to ask questions. The reality you saw is the reason for you to respond whether you are saying yes, asking a question or warning the writer that you are not going to spend a cent. Whenever a scam proposal responder asks questions, he or she creates an avenue for further pressure to be applied if the writer is indeed a scammer. The responder might finally be convinced to go into the business. You never know.

What scam proposal responders do not know is that, **all responses establish contact.** The Scammer does not get scam targets' contacts easily, so when a scam target responds to a scam proposal, the scammer now confirms the real contact information and can always reach the scam target with further convincing information. Also, there is still the possibility that another scam proposal might interest the scam target in the future, as long as the scam target has established real contact information by responding to the proposal. The scammer simply sees it as; money transfer scam might not be for the target but the lottery winning scams might interest the target. It is important to note that the content of the scam target's first response does not matter much to the seasoned scammer.

In most scam stories I have studied, I believe that every scam proposal responder somehow fancied the business, somehow that responder believed such a business was possible, hence the response. If the responder was so sure not to spend a cent and would never do so, no matter what, why waste time responding and waiting for the scammer's payment requests only for you to say you will not make payment. Time spent, email costs, telephone costs, etc., are not worth it if you were so sure it was a scam from the beginning to be honest, unless you were doing some research on the subject. In reality, many scam proposal responders are sure prospective scam victims; sooner or later they will comply when the right scam proposal come calling. This sequence has more than 50% compliance from scam stories I have come across. The majority of these scam victims claim to have known what scam was before they got scammed.

The normal storyline from frequent scam proposal responder who finally became a scam victim is always:

'I know scams but this one looked different.'

'It sounded so real; I even spoke to his mother.'

'I know scams but I thought I was helping someone in need.'

'I was doing it for the sake of charity.'

'I was not interested in my share of the money; I just wanted to help them.'

'He said he lived in the UK.'

'He called me with a United States number.'

Even Mr. Ojo above, who responded **'go to hell with your business',** had made his contact details available to the scammer to keep sending other proposals, believing that a different kind of proposal might interest Mr. Ojo and it might. Mr. Ojo might fall for a different charity or credit card scam. You never know.

Have you ever wondered why some people fall victim to lottery scams but not for money transfer scams? You should understand that the scammer believes every responder to a scam proposal is a potential victim who will surely go into a scam business one day, when the right, matching scam proposal come calling.

I also observed that most prospective scam victims who ask questions in their responses to scam proposals might not even be very sure of the answers to their questions. When you ask questions about something that is new to you, such as most scams proposals are to their targets, then, you have entered the process of learning from the scammer (teacher or director)—The scammer will of course teach you to his or her advantage. On the other hand, when you ask the questions to which you already know the answers, you have appointed yourself the examiner and the scammer your student—students (scammers) can still pass your almighty exam. When they pass, what's next? You might deal!

Another problem in responding to scam proposal and asking any questions is that you must be sure that the expected answer is correct and that your communication content does not expose your expected answer. Moreover, the answer the scammer provides might distort your focus on the expected answer you are waiting for. This is clearly manifested in the answer the scammer gave to Mr. Saleh above; the perfect Oxford

University alumni answer seems to have replaced the five-page scam publication question. All these risks are there when you reply to a scam proposals. You might even act unconsciously to regret it later.

C. NEGATIVE RESPONSE TO SCAM PROPOSALS

In this type of scam proposal response, there is actually no response. Only when the scam target does not respond to the scam proposal or scam scheme is there a negative response. Any reply or response cannot be negative; it is either a positive response or an intermediate response. When you ignore a scam proposal or scam scheme you have responded negatively to that proposal. The scammers might continue to send more and different scam proposals, and you still do not respond; you have actually shown that you are not interested. This is the only way to indicate no interest. It will cost you nothing and you are not interested, period!

A scammer employing random sampling of a scam proposal, sending 2 million emails and getting no reply will be very demoralized. A scammer whose phone calls are dropped 100 times in a day will feel bad. A scam HYIP websites that has no investor for a year might be pulled down by the scammer. Of course, these scammers might start thinking twice about their scam businesses. Any kind of response gives hope to the scammer. This is one thing responders of scam proposals must realize. After all, no-one knows every scam. Scams and scammers can come in different forms, different medium and introduce different proposals. Even genuine businesses can transform into scams. This is why it is important for one to understand clearly the features of a scam business; Part 3.

Most people respond to events as they perceive them. One has to be careful in deciphering reality from unreality. Ignoring the suspicious scam proposal or scam scheme is always the best way to avoid scams. Every scam proposal I analyzed had a deadline and when the target did not reply, the scammer's scheme must change. The scammer will start changing wordings, dates, deadlines, amounts, information, etc., in the proposal, just to get the target's attention in the form of a response or payment.

I receive about 30-50 scam proposals in my emails weekly. I respond to none mostly, because I know they are scam proposals. At times I may respond when the proposal is very unique and I want to know the scammer's scheme. This has always been my routine for several years now, until I got one a few months ago that showed me another phase to this advanced game. It was a domain name scam of another kind.

The email was addressed to my company, the writer claimed to be working for an organization based in China that registers domain names. The writer wanted to notify me that my company's domain name was being requested by another company. This new company wanted to register . . . *mycompanyname.net* while my company is . . . *mycompanyname.com*. The writer politely asked if I did not mind to allow this new company register this domain name or I could reserve for life all such domains including all the *.net, .org, .info, .us, .co.uk, etc.* It was very reasonable for a fee of $500 for life. This meant that no one else could ever register any domain name similar to mine. The writer was polite and decent, so I accepted to go ahead.

The writer wanted payment by Western Union which was the first mistake; my suspicion began to be aroused, although it did not bother me much. I told him I needed more time, saying I would send him the money after the weekend. He said it was okay, giving a Wednesday deadline for my payment or he would allow the other company to register a similar domain name to mine. On the Wednesday when I told him I still didn't have the money, he gave me another Monday deadline. I now smelled a rat and kept him on hold. He kept shifting his deadlines. It is now several months later as I write this story and he has just given me another deadline. These deadline shifts just showed me it was a scam and I have ignored him since then.

I have never seen a scam so well planned as this one with all my exposure. I have not explained the whole story in its every detail, but it was a classic. It looked very real and genuine, but it was a scam. I would have paid the $500 no doubt, the only problem was that I was watching the business process, and the process I saw was a clear scam, featuring frequent deadline rescheduling. *(See Chapter 22, Part 3)*.

Notice that even when I responded unknowingly to this domain name scam, my knowledge of the features of scam businesses saved me from losing $500, which is what is important to remember.

All the convincing from the domain name scammer above was because I responded to the proposal. If I had not responded, I would not have come that close to losing my $500.

Do not assume you might know how to go about it. ***Any proposal anyone suspects is a scam should be ignored.***

Your instinct can guide you. The moment you smell it, make effort to believe it, it will be a scam. Do not waste your time even replying, I wonder what you think your response will achieve, apart from inviting further persuasion from the scammer in trying to make you reconsider and go into the business. If you mistakenly respond or must respond due to the proposal's nature, make sure you are very knowledgeable in the scam business features as explained in Part 3 of this book.

CHAPTER 13

TYPES OF ENTRY INTO SCAM BUSINESSES

Many scam targets entered the scams differently. Scam targets become prospective victims and eventual scam victims in many different ways after receiving the scam proposals. Our individual differences contribute to this because each scam target might have a different reason for entering the scam business. Even where all targets wanted to make easy money as the sole reason, the possibility that they all had different designs for the money is still there. All these differences put together psychologically influence each target's approach to the scam business.

Irrespective of the medium in which the scam proposal was presented and the type of scam it was, a scam target can become a prospective scam victim or scam victim in a scam business or scheme accidentally, unknowingly, and knowingly.

A. ACCIDENTAL ENTRY VICTIMS:

Many victims entered into the scams accidentally. They came for something genuine that later on became a scam. In accidental entry, the victims neither bought the offer in the scam proposals nor fancied it. They were not interested in any of the promised gain in the scam proposal. These victims were not pursuing any profit but somehow they are in business with the scammers, have paid the scammers or lost money to the scams. Good examples on how one can enter into scan businesses accidentally are fake websites, Scam websites can resemble genuine websites and in most cases you might think you were dealing with the right entity; identity theft (phishing), stolen credit cards, unsolicited email links, etc. You lost money to scammers not because you were in a business with them to gain but because they accidentally got your information or you accidentally ran into their scheme. In accidental scam business entry, the victim is decent and does not pretend otherwise.

This type of victim will quit the whole business on the slightest hint that the business is a scam. He or she will ask the suspected scammer no questions and expect no answers.

B.   UNKNOWN ENTRY VICTIMS:

You can enter a purported profitable business without knowing it was a scam. The majority of scam victims entered the scams unknowingly. Such victims are business like; they like profit and making more money. They got scammed mostly because of wanting to make more money and misinformation. This form of entry is quite different from the accidental entry, because here the victims' imaginations of the gains to be made in these businesses brought them into the scam. They were aiming to make more money like in a genuine business venture, but unbeknownst to them this particular business was a scam. You accepted to go into the business, there was something for you to gain, and you opened a communication with a business partner, but did not know this business partner was a scammer.

It is also important to note that some genuine businesses are scam prone in their business process. As the business started, the victim never suspected it was a scam until the business processes started manifesting fully and the scam features started presenting themselves. Most internet scams are unknown; get-quick-rich schemes are scams you can enter unknowingly. When victims enter scam businesses unknowingly, they are quick to stop further spending, payments or investments and curtail further communications with the scammer once the scammer cannot remove their doubts. Such victim's questions must be accurately answered by the suspected scammer if the victim is to remain in the business. Also note that the majority of these unknown entry victims' questions originate from changes in their anticipated business process. What they anticipated will happen in the business have changed so they ask questions. They need explanation from the suspected scammer. The scammer will keep trying to answer the victims' questions until the victim's 'desired' answers are provided. **Also note that,** *it is still possible to provide the right answer for such victims who entered the scam business via unknown entry.* The victims in this kind of entry might be sure or unsure of the answers to their questions, but unless the suspected scammer provides a satisfying answer, which might not necessarily be the right answer, the suspected scammer will never be able to scam such victims further.

Unknown entry victims might have been paying the scammer, but any deviation from their anticipation as another business development will put doubt into their minds, which must be cleared. The majority of scam victims worldwide fall into this group; many scam victims said they asked a given question, and were given the "desired" answer before they went on with the business.

This type of victim will ask questions but must wait for the answers from the suspected scammer. They will quit the business if the suspected scammer cannot provide their 'desired answer' to their satisfaction.

C. KNOWN ENTRY VICTIMS:

This classifies the prospective victims who know exactly what they are doing from the date they receive the scam proposal. Known entry is classified into two categories. The first comprises those victims who are fully aware that the *business is illegal* and they still proceeded. The second category is composed of those who are fully aware of what scams are, but this time, the particular *scam proposal presentation was different*, deceiving them into going into the business.

In the first group, their subconscious screamed 'illegality', 'illegal business or 'theft', which they ignored. These types of scam victims heard the warning clearly, but as criminals themselves, their self-confidence made them believe they could outsmart the illegality. As criminals they know what they are doing; how they will launder the money, redistribute, invest, and hide the funds, etc. They have powerful connections to carry out most illegal businesses and keep the illegal gains safe. They are fully aware that what they want to do in conjunction with their business partner (scammer) who sent them the proposal is illegal. The only difference here is that they did not know that the business partner is a scammer and no profit is coming. These kinds of scam victims are very common in 'money transfer scams' and 'wash money scam'; they also make-up a good majority of high paying scam victims. Known entry scam victims are illegal experts, they are full of confidence and they pay scammers the highest amounts. They have all the needed contacts for laundering any amount of money. They own big businesses, and large magnitude businesses are not strange to them, but they were not aware that the new business with this other partner was a scam, and that there will be no illegal gains for them to launder or hide for anyone this time. We will regard these kinds of entries as *known* because the victims knew what they were doing was illegal, but not a scam. Some illegal businesses and scam businesses have resemblances we will discuss in Chapter 28—*Legalities and Illegalities.*

The second category in known entry victims are those victims who entered the scam business because it seemed different from previous scams of which they were aware. This means that these victims were fully aware of what scams are, but because this particular proposal was different, they believed it. The difference probably was in the proposal's source, the introductory medium, country mentioned, or the business process that ensued was different from what they have heard about scams. Also probably, the scam proposal was in their native language or from a close relation, so they decided to let down their guard and proceed with the business, which eventually became a scam.

You have always heard of the 'Nigerian 419' money transfer scam letter but you fell for another money transfer scam letter from Kuala Lumpur (Malaysia). You are fully aware of 'money transfer' scams but you fell for a 'wash money' scam. You know very well that many HYIPs are fakes but you fell for another HYIP because their headquarters was in New York according to their website. You know everything about investment scams but when you beloved brother requested your assistance in defining that investment business you assisted financially and otherwise. You have read so much and know so much about scams but you fell for a charity scam in your backyard. You are fully aware of 'cold call scams' but you fell for same 'cold call scam' because the caller said he was from your bank. It just goes on and on. Many enter scam businesses solely because, one minor thing differed either in the scam business proposal, or in the ensuing scam business process, from what they have heard or read about scams. This was the only reason why these victims got scammed. Scam presentations and processes differ, so it is better for everyone to understand the features of scam businesses and not just be aware of a few scam presentations types.

Therefore, in known entry into scam:

- ***Some victims knew exactly from day one that it was an illegal business, corruption or theft, but they still proceeded knowing the risks.***

- *Some victims were fully aware from day one that the business proposal is suspicious, but because the storyline of this new proposal slightly differed from what they had heard previously or what they were aware of, they entered the scam.*
- *Some victims anticipated a particular business process to ensure based on their previous knowledge which differed from what they knew, so they fell into the trap.*

When victims enter scams businesses knowingly as the case may be, they go into the scam business with vigor because these victims have already asked themselves some questions that they have answered to their satisfaction. It is this kind of victims who refuse to leave the business, and act strangely because they have inbuilt trust into the business, due to their previous knowledge. These victims ask themselves and their suspected scammers the questions, but these victims also provide the majority of their 'desired' answers. Such victims provide answers to their questions to justify their next payments to the scammers. These victims seem hypnotized by the business as they keep providing themselves answers to their doubts. In known entry into a scam, signals that the business is a scam will come to these victims but they will answer these queries themselves with reasons that mainly satisfy them because of their previous knowledge. Their previous knowledge is always their greatest shortcomings.

I have read where some of these victims even say 'let them test their business partner with this little money first'. As a matter of fact, I wonder what you are testing a scammer with little money for. Other victims are so rich that a little withdrawal from their bank balance does not matter much, so they proceed and are excited going into such scam businesses. A good percentage of high paying scam victims have a known entry into scam.

It is also worthy of note that unknown entry scams victims can develop into known entry scams; when the victim becomes fully aware of what the business entails and still he or she pursues it.

In known entry, a big percentage of the victims' suspicions are alleviated or cleared by the victims themselves.

Look at this situation for instance;

A scam victim in 'wash money' scam expecting cash money payment in Scotland from South Africa might be wondering how

such an amount of cash in a big trunk box can be transported through Europe, passing the strict authorities in European borders. Same victim will answers himself or herself when the so called couriers transporting the said big trunk box calls with a European telephone number that they are now in Europe. There ends the victim's questions and suspicions, as the next scam process stage begins.

I have come across this scenario in scam stories severally. A European telephone number seems to have cleared the victim's doubts on how such an amount of cash could be transported past customs and immigrations in Europe. The victim's legitimate question has been answered by the call. The call has only posed as an answer because the question remained unanswered.

A victim who has no previous knowledge of such illegal border crossings will continue to doubt how those couriers did pass the border but a known entry victim will reason; 'why still bother about how they crossed the border when they are already here'. They see no illegality in such crossings as long as business proceeds.

An unknown entry victim in similar instance as above will be surprised and the courier must give a tangible answer of how they crossed the border or no business. Likewise, the unknown entry scam victim can believe that the border security was bribed and even contribute part of the bribe. An accidental entry scam victim, on the other hand, will quit the whole business as soon as the scammers mention that they will cross the border with such an amount of cash. Imagine what would have happened to that scam if all victims insisted on knowing in details how those couriers crossed the border with the trunk box.

In both types of known entry, the victims' past knowledge somehow assist their reasoning in tolerating illegalities.

HYIP Investors wondering how the HYIP makes money to pay investors such promised high returns on their investments will naturally stop asking these questions when their own so called investment returns are genuinely credited to their own accounts. That line of questioning will not be necessary again, what will become necessary is how to take good advantage of the opportunity by investing more in that very same HYIP.

Follow a big scam story meticulously and you will notice that, the next development in the scamming process always dissolves the victim's last doubt, or rather the latest development in a scam business process has a way of clearing the victim's qualms in that particular business.

Scams reach the stage where this occurrences of new developments, become the business.

This type of victim in known entry will ask questions and provide the answers, too, by assuming business progresses are the answers. These victims will only quit the business when there are no possible new developments or the scammer cannot move to the next business stage.

When you ask questions and also provide the answers, then you are asking yourself the questions and your business partner is not obliged to give you answers.

CHAPTER 14

COMMITMENTS IN SCAM BUSINESSES

A major process in scam business is the scam victim's commitment to the scam business. Apart from the introduction, the response, and the payments to the scammer, which we will discuss later, commitment is one major process in all scams that can be easily misunderstood as it can be hidden or exposed. Commitment from the scam victim is a major contributor to the success of most scams. The problem also is that the majority of scam victims and most authorities fighting scams never really understand what commitment to a scam business is, and the different kinds of commitments that can be exhibited in a business, whether scam or not.

Commitment is what makes the scam victim spend millions unnecessarily in a business relationship with an unknown person that the police and authorities find difficult to understand. *'You paid someone you have not seen before a million dollars?'* This occurs because the payer was committed to whatever business it was. Authorities ignore the scam victim's commitment to the scam business and keep wondering how the scam victim paid millions in a simple business relationship that was based on some phone calls or probably on simple documents the scam victim has.

When you understand the commitment, then you will be able to solve this riddle. If the scam victim is not committed to the scam business or the scam scheme, the scammer will not be able to extort money or information from that victim. It is only in few rare cases that a victim pays a scam scheme without being committed, or respectfully, I would rather say that all scam victims are committed or were committed to different levels in the scam businesses that scammed them.

There are different kinds of commitments that can come into play in a scam business in progress.

A. ORDINARY COMMITMENT IN SCAMS:

This type of commitment in scam business emerges first after the scam target becomes a prospective scam victim by responding to or complying with the scam proposal. Because the prospective victim has given a positive response or accepted to go into the business, there is something the prospective victim is expected to do. In some cases it might be an online registration, registration form completion, provision of contact address and contact numbers, answering the scammer's calls, reading the scammer's emails, storing your business partner's (scammer's) contact details in your phonebook, recognizing the scammer's voice on the phone and so many others. This is the preliminary commitment expected if the prospective victim has agreed to go into the business. At least a line of communication between the prospective victim and the scammer in this case must be established. In serious cases, depending on the type of scam, this ordinary commitment might require the victim getting a new email address, releasing private telephone numbers, submitting bank details, calling back, checking the scammer's emails regularly, etc. Ordinary commitment costs the prospective victim nothing or next to nothing, just dedication and the release of vital information for indicating interest to participate in the business. *The prospective victim is expected to be ordinarily committed, for the business to be possible by all ramifications.* The scammer might give directives to make the victim ordinarily committed but it lies on the prospective victim to assure the business partner (unknown scammer) that his or her end of the business is fully covered as they look forward to the promised gain.

The ordinary commitment does not guarantee that the prospective victim will incur expenses or make payments to the scammer or any other party,

Ordinary commitment is also seen in most genuine business transactions. In scam business transactions, this commitment level indicates that the prospective victim is ready to go into the business. I also noted that in scam business ordinary commitment, the prospective victim might not necessarily be returning the scammer's calls but will comfortably take the scammer's calls. Ordinary commitment is the foremost commitment of every willing business partner in genuine business and every prospective scam victim in scam business. For instance, in a scam business, if for every time the scammer call, the prospective victim does not recognize who is on the line, then the ordinary commitment is lacking. A closer observation will show you that the calling business partner will always complain seriously about this and will do anything possible to ensure this basic ordinary commitment is in place. Some scam websites even have counters and visitor monitors that keep records, to know exactly how many times a particular visitor has visited the website. This is all designed in a bid to know the visitor's ordinary commitment level.

Generally, ordinary commitment is in all business transactions. After all, it will be improper for the business (scam or not) to go wrong from any participant's side having indicated interest. This is also what develops ordinary commitments in the prospective scam victims in scam businesses.

B. BUSINESS COMMITMENT IN SCAMS:

During business commitment in scam businesses, the prospective victim has started incurring noticeable expenses to ensure that the business goes through. These expenses will start to occur consciously and unconsciously. Likewise, the same prospective victim is consciously and unconsciously adding up these expenses, believing that the promised gain will replenish them. Business commitment in a scam business resembles normal business commitment; the prospective victim has now started complying with the fact that business has costs and profits. Prospective victim in scam businesses also perceives the situation as so. Some examples of such business commitments are; opening a new online payment account, a new bank account, securing a new private telephone number, securing a new fax number, sending your signed letterhead paper, registering a new company name for the business, getting an identity card or international passport, and the prospective victim renegotiating distribution of the promised gain. Any action that will involve tangible expenses or payments, done by the prospective victim in scam business to make conditions ideal for the business is scam business commitment. Business commitment in scam costs the prospective victim some money, time or effort. Definitely, the prospective victim foregoes something somehow in scam business commitment.

It was while analyzing a scam victim's detailed story that I realized it was because of the business commitment that the scam victim started asking the scammer certain questions like 'when' and 'how' the business will be concluded, etc. In business commitment in scam businesses, the prospective scam victim has started investing noticeable time and money, the scammer might or might not know about, so there is a need for that prospective victim to be sure of every business step henceforth. At this stage of commitment in scam business; imaginations of the promised gain have started creeping into the prospective victim's consciousness. Likewise, the victim, judging from the business processes so far, has started nursing the realization that the business might be a success. Therefore, the prospective victim is now doing business; business costs are involved, there will be profit, as promised by the scammer, and, if possible, the prospective victim would like to know the financial and business layout of this business (scam) which will manifest as questions of 'when' and 'how' to the business partner (scammer).

Business commitment in scam businesses, guarantees that the prospective victim will incur expenses or make payments but not necessarily to the scammer. This is because such payments can be made to other parties than the scammer. Examples are; the prospective victim might make payments to the telephone company for the new line or to the company registry for the new company registration as business costs. The prospective victim can also buy a new fax machine and pay the electronic shop directly, which expense the scammer might not be aware of. Prospective victims in a scam business who are business committed will incur expenses and spend time, which they will term 'business costs' in conditioning their side for the business they do not know is a scam. Never forget that based on the promised gain in the scam proposal, the prospective victim is also subconsciously recording these noticeable expenses he or she is incurring, thereby, increasing the overall commitment in the business. These commitments will later appear when the scam victim's reasoning will claim to have earned—the business success and the promised gain.

You will discover that business commitment in scam business, where the prospective victim has started incurring expenses as business costs that, supposedly, the promised gain will replenish is also common in genuine businesses. But, uniquely, in scam businesses, the scammer's skill is used to re-direct these business costs (expenses) developed in business commitment or, at least, some of these business costs, which the prospective victim is incurring in business commitment, to become payments to the scammer. The re-direction of business costs to be payments to the scammer is the targeted commitment the scammer desires.

C. TARGETED COMMITMENT:

This is the final commitment the scammer wants and has been chasing from day one of sending the scam proposal to the scam target. Targeted commitment is the commitment level whereby the prospective victim in a scam is now comfortable with making business expenses and payments directly to the scammer or following the scammer's directives without any suspicion. The trust has now been built and the victim sees nothing wrong in sending monies (business cost payments) to a business partner (scammer) as long as the business partner (scammer) reports back that the purpose of the money was accomplished or done successfully.

In every ongoing scam business, the scammer's chase for targeted commitment from the victim is a major characteristic of scam businesses, it is very pronounced in any scam business whether successful or in progress. The scammers will make all possible and concerted efforts to direct business expenses to themselves. Scammers will chase targeted commitment so tactically that most victims will never notice.

Target commitment can eventuate when, for example, the scammer advises an unsuspecting victim to appoint an attorney the scammer knows well to represent the victim in signing papers, instead of the victim traveling to sign those papers personally. The idea sounds reasonable in avoiding risks, but the scammer, in this example, is trying to divert the business cost of signing papers to himself or herself through a lawyer (scammer's partner), instead of the victim paying the same amount of money for travel ticket and accommodation to sign the papers personally. The scammer as the only person with the knowledge that the business is a scam, will not allow such waste as travel expense for signing papers he or she is fully aware are worthless papers—for there is no business in a scam. Another example of the scammer directing business commitment to become targeted commitment is the scammer telling the victim that he or she will assist in raising part of the money required for an established business expenses in the business. One objective here is to ensure that the victim does not pay another person out of instinct by keeping a close watch. It is natural for the victim to inform the scammer, as a fellow contributor, once the victim's part of the contribution is ready.

These directives and rerouting of business expenses will become frequent as the scam progresses, and the moment the scammer starts to achieve these kinds of successes with the victim, then the scam has matured, the prospective victim is now a real scam victim as the targeted commitment is fully in place. Targeted commitment is further elaborated in Chapter 18 as a feature of scam business in Part 3.

D. SCAM BUSINESS LOYALTY AND DISLOYALTY:

Let us look into this issue of loyalty and disloyalty because it has a good resemblance with commitment to a cause, particularly a business cause in this instance.

A loyal person is one who is faithful to somebody, something, a cause or an ideal while a disloyal person is one showing a lack of faith in somebody or something. Loyalty and disloyalty to a cause is often underestimated until the damage has become irreparable. So many people are committed to businesses they do not know are full scale scam and they will never disclose their involvement to anyone, no matter how close their relationship is with that person.

A person's natural loyalty plays a major role in the aspect of that person's commitment in business ventures, including scams. Some people were brought up to be loyal to anything they are convinced of. In scam business stories, I have observed, that the loyalty and disloyalty of participating partners reside in our perceptions of these terms. This is true and easily misunderstood. Bear in mind that a loyal person does not necessarily mean that such a person is an honest or a good person. Likewise, being a disloyal person does not necessarily mean he or she is a dishonest person or a bad person. Loyalty and disloyalty are defined in reference to faith or belief in somebody or something—belief in a cause or disbelief in that cause—lacking faith in a certain process or having confidence in a system. Fundamentalism found in religions have basis in loyalty.

It is not easy to make a fundamentalist out of an unbeliever.

As a matter of fact, scammers I have observed are loyal in their scam businesses to their own advantage, whereas a scam victim or prospective scam victim's loyalty to a business is dangerous if that business is a scam. On the other hand, if the business is a scam, a prospective victim's disloyalty is an added advantage in not being easily scammed. A totally unbelievable reverse to normal business practice because the business in this very case is a scam.

The greatest scams the world has heard were those played on loyal, serious-minded and dedicated individuals, who are known to be fully focused on any venture they dare enter into.

On the other hand*, a disloyal person is not so easily scammed.* If a prospective victim is disloyal; does not follow the scammer's instruction and always give the impression that he or she has no faith that the business will succeed will really bother the scammer. This is so because the scammer's real intentions are based solely on the prospective victim having faith in the ongoing business, that way, the scammer will be able to extort money from the victim.

The independent spirit of very confident persons is a major player in loyalty. 'I have decided on what to do and so shall it be, period'. The very intelligent one minded thinker. If you happen to know a loved one with this mind set, it is important you keep a close watch before such a person enters into a scam and keeps it confidential, which he or she will definitely do, claiming to know what they are doing as a very confident person.

A loyal person demands no persuasion. He or she is fully convinced in the heart of anything they are involved in. When finally convinced for a go ahead, a loyal person's commitment to any venture is of the highest known order. Such a person as a prospective scam victim in a scam business might initially ask all the possible questions which the scammer might coincidentally be able to answer correctly, but once convinced with the scammer's answers, he or she will go all out for the business, doing exactly as told by the scammer.

It is also this loyalty that manifests in societies, making it possible for a crooked sect leader to instruct his or her followers to commit heinous crimes or even suicide that they do so willingly.

Loyal persons have someone or something they look up to. In scams stories, I observed that the scammer assumes the position of someone to look up to subconsciously to the scam victim. This position the scammer assumes can be arrogated to the fact that the scammer is the initiator of the business (unknown scam) with an upcoming gain both of them (scammer and victim) will benefit. Therefore, the prospective victim is easily open to the scammer, at times exposing his or her entire nature unknowingly to the scammer. Additionally, the scammer has the advantage of privileged information; because only the scammer is aware that the business in which they are involved is a scam and will never materialize. So, while loyalty moves followers, the leader (scammer) controls followers (victims).

In most scams stories, scam publication and even scam schemes on the internet, you can deduce that the scammer assumed the driver's position, directing what is right and wrong. Likewise, directing what should be done or not done. The unsuspecting victim follows the scammer's directives as a loyal follower.

Lastly, the loyalty of the prospective victim/victim in scams is based on emotions not principles as expected in genuine business relationships. The abnormal imagination of the scam victim in a paying scam matures emotionally. This is why even a person, who is very strict naturally and does not tolerate flimsy excuses even from loved ones, when in a scam business will keep tolerating unnecessary excuses from the scammer; why another payment is required for upgrade, and so on, why the consignment did not arrive, why there is no traffic in the website, why the bank is using a different number, why you did not get the call, why the program will pay next week, why another payment has to be made, etc.

The loyalty of a person to a business is a total disadvantage if that business is a scam as the loyalty will only cause more harm. The same is applicable to anyone who has absolute loyalty to an organization that has evil or dishonest intentions.

The only problem with anything secret (secret business, secret organization or a secret arrangement) is that, it takes just one bad leader of the said secret venture to change the purpose of such a venture, even if the initial purpose of such a secret venture was honorable. Based on all participants' loyalty to a joint cause as seen in scams, a scam victim in a scam business is like one in a secret arrangement and the scammer is the leader of this secret venture, chasing a promised gain.

CHAPTER 15

POSSIBLE PAYMENTS IN SCAM BUSINESSES

There are many types of payments the scam victim pays in a scam business. We will treat the monetary losses of the prospective victims or victims as business expenses, because the victim that expended was of the belief that he or she was in a business, where a promised gain (profit) was to materialize later as seen in genuine business situations.

We have already discussed in commitments, how the scammer tries to use any skill possible in getting these business expenses as payments to be made to him or her by the scam victim. I have likewise observed that some payments made by the scam victim encouraged the other payments and portrayed the personality or integrity of the paying victim to the scammer. In avoiding scams, you must try to analyze your expenses in any business to see if they are scam payments.

Analyses indicate that most payments made by the unsuspecting victims in a scam business fall into three groups of scam payments.

A. DISCHARGE PAYMENTS:

These are mainly minor payments the scam victim makes either to the scammer or to other entities that will somehow benefit the prospective victim or victim immediately or later on, should the business go wrong. Since they will somehow benefit the prospective victim, the prospective victim is quick in making these discharge payments. A good example is buying a new telephone line for a business that is a scam. The telephone line is still yours whether the proposed business it was meant for works out or not; you still have your telephone line for other uses. Opening an online payment account or bank account are other examples of discharge payments. The online payment accounts for example; MoneyBookers (Skrill), PayPal, Liberty Reserve, Perfect Money, etc., still remains yours afterwards, whether the business worked out or not, because you used genuine IDs to open these accounts.

Making a $10 trial investment in a suspicious HYIP is also a discharge payment, since you will gain further knowledge from that first $10 test investment. The $10 investment will inform you whether to proceed with higher investments or cease future investments in that HYIP. The $10 HYIP investment example is tricky and commonly misunderstood. Most victims will fall for such test payments and do not really understand why.

If you will carefully study most scams on the internet, telephone, mails, etc., you will discover that the scam scheme designers must now include the 'discharge payment' investor's level for those prospective victims who must test the system to be convinced before they make larger investments.
The majority of scams on the internet now take this shape.

The amount set to attract discharge payments is normally very small and works successfully. These scammers employ the technique that so many small amounts from many people will become a big amount. This is the new trend in these scams appearing almost everywhere on the internet. The effectiveness of discharge payments should not be underestimated, because, the internet and other communication mediums have made it easier to reach millions of people with a click, multiplying possible returns on such discharge payments that the majority of people who come across the scam scheme will make. $10 discharge payment from 100,000 people is $1,000,000.

Discharge payments in investment scams are very unique and an art because the scammer can gain or lose, such as the victim can gain or lose. Both parties are carefully watching and studying the other's reactions on a $10 investment for instance. It is clear that both parties can forgo $10 which poses no problems for these two, although the scammer still has a higher advantage. If the investor is paid the investment return, say $3 after three days, the investor can withdraw the whole $13 and not invest again, so the HYIP owner (scammer) loses. If the investor is paid and he or she reinvests $13, as the scammer is expecting, then the game is still on. You must never forget that the scammer's game in an investment scam still has expiration time when the scammer cannot sustain the deal further and must take the investors' monies. It will then depend on what stage of investment the investor (victim) is in. Consider $10 from 500 discharge payment investors is $5000 and some good cash for the scam HYIP owner. The scam scheme can be over at this stage. The scammer's continuation of the scam HYIP is dependent on the prospects of the present HYIP investors which the scammer is also monitoring. I am guilty of these test investments, being discharge payments, and I initially lost a lot of money before I realized what was going on.

Mainly, it is in order to gain more information about the business that many victims fall for discharge payment. Also note that when making such discharge payments to gain better information, the prospective victims must be sure not to be greedy or they may be paying the scam directly.

Going back to our earlier discussion, a benefit will always emanate from a prospective victim making a discharge payment. What a prospective victim expects to gain from a discharge payment depends on that victim. ***Better information on the ensuing business*** is the worst that the prospective victim can expect to gain from making discharge payments, so a prospective scam victim is quick in making discharge payments on scam schemes. Discharge payments are normally small amounts depending on what the scammer feels will be commitment enough from the scam target. It is also the scammers first way of assessing the prospective victim; knowing how rich the victim is, the victim's financial ability and other needed estimations about the prospective victim.

Discharge payment also helps the scammer in estimating the commitment level of the prospective scam victim. Discharge payments increase your commitment to the business, yet they are treated as unrecorded casual payments. You will notice that after making a $10 discharge payment on a HYIP, you will find yourself regularly checking the HYIP, which is commitment upon the meager amount you spent.

Scammers are starting to modify discharge payments to be their main scam payment, considering the multiplier effect it can have, should many unsuspecting victims pay it. The modification of discharge payment by scammers to benefit them at once is in order to scam as many people as possible, due to the internet and ease in sending scam proposals. The amount paid by the victim in discharge payments can be large sums or small amounts. It all depends on the prospective victim's financial status and the scammer's design in that particular scam.

When making discharge payments, the victim has not fully understood the processes of this new business. More than 80% of discharge payments made by victims in scam businesses are voluntary and doesn't require much persuasion from the scammers.

B. INVISIBLE PAYMENTS:

These are payments made by the prospective victims in a scam business from which the prospective victim stands to benefit nothing, but must be made if the business must continue to appear genuine to the scam victim. Likewise the scammer in a business that led the victim to make invisible payments gains nothing from the victim making invisible payments. You see in scam businesses, there is no business to start with. The prospective victims have been lured into these invisible payments unnecessarily by the scam scheme. In most cases, the scammer is quick in stopping these kinds of payments where possible, since the scammer stands to gain nothing from the victim making such invisible payments. Scammers unavoidably allow the victim to make invisible payments if they encourage further commitment from the prospective victim to their business cause.

Invisible payments being normal day to day payments are very logical to the prospective victim and the scammer handles such matters with extreme care. I have repeatedly observed this when acting the victim. A scammer trying to alter the process of an invisible payment can make even the dumbest of prospective victims suspicious and can ruin the whole scam scheme. Invisible payments are also payments spent on scam businesses that most scam victims will not count on, even when reporting scams to the authorities.

Examples of invisible payments are telephone bills, membership fees, transportation bills, bank charges, money transfer charges, online commissions, service charges, bank COT, taxes, and facility fees paid, etc. Scam victims hardly mention these as payments they made, when complaining to have been scammed.

Clearly, the primary purpose of a scam is for the scammer to extort money from the prospective victim, which he or she can only do if the prospective victim believes the business is genuine. Invisible payments make scams appear genuine and many scams schemes are now employing it. I have observed that many scammers purposely put in invisible payments to add credibility to their scams. A good example is a scammer telling the scam victim that his or her international passport is a must for the business. If the prospective victim does not have one and spends some money (invisible payment) to secure an international passport for the business, the scammer has added credibility to the scam scheme. This is so because a cost that is official or governmental has been added to the unknown business scheme. Moreover, the money was not paid to the scammer. It was paid to a genuine government agency in charge of issuing international passports. Another good example that can result into an invisible payment is an investment scam set up, requesting for your official ID for registration or withdrawal. The ID request only adds credibility to the business process and does not mean that the business cannot still be a scam.

Invisible payments are also common in genuine business processes, so they are not strange to most prospective scam victims. In scam businesses, invisible payments, no matter how logical to the victims, are also wastes because there is no business in a scam. A clear example is the bank charges for wiring funds overseas. The bank will automatically deduct their charges from the victim's account to wire the funds. Most prospective victims will treat such bank charges as casual, yet it involved a big sum of money paid to the bank. In avoiding scams, one must realize that monies spent by the victims on the scam businesses were also payments by the victims. Another example of invisible payment is the victim's telephone bill increasing from $25 monthly to $700. Many scam victim rarely consider the cause of this increase, neither will they mention such as scam payments to anyone. I also believe that all invisible expenses are being added subconsciously in the victim's mind, leading to further commitment to the business.

Some things common in invisible payments are; the scammer has no way to benefit from this payment and might jeopardize the whole scam scheme in an effort to gain from invisible payments. Invisible payments can be made by the prospective victim at any time; it can be before, during and after the scam scheme has been fully downloaded onto the prospective victim. More than 80% of invisible payments are involuntary; neither the victim nor scammer could control or stop these invisible payments, if the scam scheme was to continue appearing as a genuine business to the unsuspecting victim—Your business partner (scammer) cannot stop you from paying you taxes or telephone bills.

C. FINALE PAYMENTS:

Finale payment is that payment made by the victim in a scam business that supposedly will remove any business success snags and materialize the promised gain. Finale payments are normally requested by the scammer and the scammer can also scheme the scam to lead to a final payment request. Initially, it will appear as one payment but will become many as the scam progresses. In real scams, finale payments will keep appearing repeatedly and the majority of scam victims will never notice this sequence of re-appearing finale payments to be followed by the expected gain as promised by the scammers. Instead, most scam victims will interpret finale payments as **problem solvers** and *solution makers.* Final payment and its request is the harvest of targeted commitment of the scam victim.

Scammers give good reasons for finale payment requests; they are well explained to the victim and likewise very logical to a paying scam victim. Finale payment requests have no end in a scam business and will continue to reappear as long as the prospective victim still believes in the business and has the required targeted commitment.

Finale payments and their requests are the main art of the scammers and where the scammers reap the targeted commitments from their victims. All that trust in the unknown business partner, if the business is a scam is bottled in finale payments. At this scam stage, the victim now trusts sending money to the scammer and expects only an answer; the purpose of sending the money has been accomplished. Finale payment is the scammer's real art of extortion. At this business stage in any scam, the scammer will now and continuously scheme all further business processes of the business (scam) to always lead to a success snag that will require monetary input (finale payment) from the victim to clear for the promised gain to materialize.

Some things common to finale payments are; finale payment requests do not end. Business success snags to be solved by finale payment somehow regenerate, soon after the last finale payment was made. Finale payments do not have a final payment in scam businesses; *each is a Finale Payment but none is a Final Payment.* Finale payment being the clearest feature of scam business is further explained in Chapter 21 part 3.

Summarily, there are instances where these different kinds of payments intertwine; you have discharge payments and invisible payments looking alike. The distinguishing fact in understanding them better, is that one should check who will gain after making that particular payment; can the victim gain in any way during and after the business whether scam or not from that payment. You will also notice that the scammers are always very careful in invisible payments; he or she will try to finalize this stage of the scamming process quickly because invisible payments can easily ruin the whole scam scheme. It is common that most prospective victims even know the person(s) responsible for invisible payments and their location. It is therefore very suspicious when the scammer tries to divert these invisible payments. It spells doom and the scammer knows this. Examples are;—**A scammer asking for the victim's telephone bills money from the victim. The scammers requesting money for paying the victims' bank charges. A scammer requesting for money in order to get an ID for the victim**

You can try to know what kind of business you are in by suggesting sending an invisible payment to your unknown business partner and watching the response. Your business partner, if a scammer, will suggest any possible alternatives to making invisible payments, but will never tell you to send the money to him or her or that he or she will assist in making invisible payments. Scammers always leave invisible payments solely to the victim. In your test, if your business partner accepts for you to send an invisible payment to them, then he or she is a scammer. Many scam victims have acknowledged these irregularities; where their so-called business partners ask them to send invisible payments to them or try to divert invisible payments, and they still proceeded with the business.

You can deduce that the scammer cannot control the emergence and payment of ordinary payments. The scammer can control the emergence of invisible payments but cannot control the payment, but the scammer can comfortably control both the emergence and payment of finale payments. Also in long lasting scams, repetition of further monetary extortions is mainly possible by finale payment requests.

Each finale payment request I repeatedly observed can be for a different purpose, as the scammer will bring in genuine payments as finale payments and also bring in strange payments as finale

payments, claiming that the strange payment requests are due to the uniqueness of the said business.

An internet work from home scam can commence; $9.99 for a daily income generating website guaranteed. You invest and no daily income is generated. You are advised to increase the number of websites, then $19 for better income websites, then $25 for the automatic robot and then $140 for the main universal traffic generating software. $19, $25 and $140 are all finale payments. The payer (victim) believed each separate payment before the next payment that followed would have brought the desired income. What started as a $9.99 discharge payment has now developed into a grand design of finale payment requests. I have purposely adhered to a money transfer scam as a victim and followed the scam process up to seven different finale payment requests from the scammers without paying any. The scammer just kept requesting for money and each time I ended up not paying, he claimed to have paid it himself or deferred it until we get the promised gain.

Finale payment request is perfected by the scammer, the grand design, and where the scammer's hope to extort the prospective victim is embedded. By the time finale payment requests will commence, the victim's targeted commitment has been assured through all the fake business processes the scammer has been adopting from the first day the victim received the scam proposal as a scam target.

A scam victim paying finale payments is deep in the scam and requires special deliverance. The commitment level of such victim is now very high. New information and discouragements might not matter much to such victim. They have come to understand the business (scam) in a different way unlike a scan victim paying discharge payments and invisible payments. Such victims upon having made discharge payments and invisible payments, can still withdraw (stop) entirely from being involved in the business without getting in too deep.

Delivering a scam victim who is paying finale payments requires serious effort because somehow such a scam victim believes in a great part of the business (scamming) process to have paid several finale payments. To rescue such a scam victim must involve re-orientation of the brain washing performed by the scammer on the victim. I believe this to be true because, even when such victim is aware the whole business is a scam and stops making finale payments, they will still read emails, reply emails, answer calls, make calls, and send faxes in relation to that same old scam business. One scam victim said it was just to inform the scammer that he will not spend a penny on the business again. The question is why still responding to same old scam business correspondences? In other words, such a victim is fully aware that no promised gain is coming in the said business because of its scam nature, what then is the reason for responding to correspondences? The reason is: often when scam victims have paid several finale payments, they start thinking they have earned the business success, which is quite different from materialization of the promised gain of the business. This subconscious feeling in a victim that the business might still materialize upon the awareness that the business is a scam is very common to victims that paid several finale payments.

Finale payments requests and compliance is the peak of scam business commitment and does not go away easily.

PART 3

FEATURES OF SCAM BUSINESSES

There are common features associated with scam businesses. These identifying signs are common in scam schemes and what a person trying to prevent being scammed should watch out for in any business. Any business venture where these features are apparent should be treated as scam, and for your business partner to prove otherwise. Everyone in an unknown business transaction is a prospective scam victim and has to be very observant to notice this features, should they manifest in the business. The manifestation of these features might differ a bit but they largely remain the same.

In this Part, we will look at these common features in scam businesses. It is also possible that the greed of the prospective victim/ victim can easily cloud the victim's vision to notice these common features or the victim is incapable of properly analyzing the business proceedings as they unfold in the business.

If you must continue the business after observing these features, then have courage to ask the right question, wait for a real answer and not a diversion instead of an answer.

CHAPTER 16

ALWAYS AN OFFER IN THE PROPOSAL

In every scam proposal there is an offer that will benefit the scam target. The confidential offer in a scam proposal is what the scam target will stand to gain. It is the offer (what to gain) that the scammer informs the unsuspecting target confidentially by a proposal. Scams can also be presented in ways that the scam target can access or figure out what they stand to gain in complying with the proposer. Written, oral or standing scam proposals can contain direct or indirect (hidden) offers.

Indirect offers are very effective because the scam target discovers it. This means that the scammer can also present conditions that will assist the target in rationalizing what he or she will gain in the business proposal. Offers in scam proposals appear as an opportunity to getting something for free. It is also common for the offer in a scam proposal to be very generous.

Direct offers can easily be detected as scam by a good number of careful people. Therefore, the scammers have been using more of indirect (hidden) offers. When the offer is hidden, for the scam target to rationalize the inbuilt gain is very effective. This as opposed to when the offer is presented directly. When the offer in a scam proposal is indirect, one of the scammer's intentions is to prompt the target to do something else that will benefit the scammer directly or indirectly.

For instance; *a simple order in a gold shop for an unavailable 'specific' design of gold jewellery can be a scam proposal with a hidden offer.*

If the above order is by a scammer, the hidden offer is to prompt the gold seller into searching for that particular gold jewelry design which the scammer might have set somewhere ready and waiting. The gold dealer might be deceived into buying that particular design jewelry someplace at a very high price, thinking that the ordering customer is a genuine buyer. This kind of scam has a hidden offer. Clearly, the ordering customer (scammer) never told the gold dealer to buy anything from anywhere in view of reselling to him or her; the scammer simply set the conditions that convinced the gold dealer that good profit can be made by completing such an order. The gold dealer having thought this out entirely, the ordering customer (scammer) can further authenticate the conditions that will prompt this particular action from a gold dealer in many ways; making a substantial deposit for the order is one of them.

The offer in every scam proposal is very attractive to most scam targets. If the target does not like the offer, then the target cannot become a prospective victim. The offer is always the distraction. It has the influence of clouding the target's reasoning, depending on the level of the target's greed. There are also offers that are so funny that I wonder how those victims actually visualized these scenarios.

How could a confirmed and seasoned millionaire business person from a well developed society believe that an average trunk box contain $50 million in cash because he or she was told so and pictures were sent to him by an unknown person? The millionaire starts investing seriously to collect the trunk box contents ($50 million in cash as told).

To understand this offer, let us analyze the above scenario in details which the scam victim never does. The highest US dollar bill in circulation is the $100 bill, $50 million worth of these $100 bills should be contained in an 'equivalent' trunk box, if you know what I mean, but the victims never think of that. The promise of getting a reasonable part of the trunk box's content plus previous monies invested and commitments so far completely blocks his judgment regarding the size of the trunk box. $50 million cash means 5,000 wraps of $10,000 each. You will need a crate or freight container to hold that much cash. Another reason for this oversight is that many people, rich men and women, have never seen huge amounts of cash money in their whole life. The cashless and credit nature of developed economies; the use of credit cards, debit cards, checks, money order, etc., is responsible for this. You will also notice that some scam victims who fell for this kind of 'wash money' scam will tell you that they were sure that the money ($50,000,000) was in the box they saw. Some victims will even swear that they saw it or counted it. How can that be?

In so many scam cases reported, some victims tried to emphasize that the offer was not the main reason why they decided to go into the business. I completely disbelieve this claim; it is not possible that one will enter into a business venture incurring expenses without any single hope of getting some gain in return. Gains vary and many things can be regarded as gains. ***Even in cases where parents paid their children's school fees, they hoped for their children to become better persons. Having responsible grownup children is a gain.***

I am unable to know or analyze what a person stood to gain in a business venture, but in the many scams stories I have come across, there was definitely something the victim hoped to gain eventually. Many victims will find it difficult to expose what they thought they would gain in order to play the righteous. What any scam victim stood to gain by going into a business that was eventually a scam is best known to that victim and only that victim can be honest about that. Self satisfaction can only be estimated and never calculated accurately by another person. Many people have done things that other people wondered what they stood to gain by doing those things.

A good name is also a gain. If the offer in the scammer's proposal is a good name, many people who want a good name will be interested, and many victims got scammed trying to achieve a good name somewhere in some charity scams. It is important to understand that what drives one person might be repulsive to another. It is relative, and I totally agree that what one person calls profit is quite different from what another person calls profit. The fact remains that in every scam that was successful, the victim in that scam was looking forward to 'something to gain' which prompted him or her to participate in the business that eventually turned out to be a scam.

The ***Initial Giving*** have been discussed in Chapter 5 and is as old as time. The initial giving in scam proposals softens the ground. The first act of generosity or honesty from the scammer is the initial giving. Even the presentation of a glorious opportunity to gain something will follow in most proposals that are scams. The modified internet scams try to explain all possible details of the offer in the business venture on their website or advert. All these work towards the great 'offer', mostly, a glorious opportunity to be rich.

It is very common in all scams that the offers in the scam proposals are blown out of ideal proportion. The scammer's proposal never misses to disproportionably enlarge the profit the scam target will get. Even when the scammer is seeking private details, he or she will also enlarge the gain you stand to get by releasing your private details.

'Invest $10 and get $25 in two days';

'You will keep 25% of the final sum that will be paid into your account';

'Earn $650 every day working from the comfort of your home';

'Fire your boss today and earn $10,000 in a week';

'Make $1 million in 6 months using our proven system'.

These are all offers and they can be scam offers. They are glorious opportunities to become rich. Whether they are scam offers will become evident as you progress into the scheme and understand the real process involved in 'fire your boss today and earn $10,000 in a week'.

Many other offers are very direct in the scam proposals, where the scammer offers to give the prospective victim some percentage of the profit for his or her assistance. Scammers will say anything in their proposals to make you participate in the business or give them assistance. Scammers can promise in their proposal to patronize your business or whatever you do, with the profit to be made in another business. 'Patronize your businesses; is a great motivator for many sellers who got scammed.

It is common for a businessman to enter a scam business because the unknown business partner (scammer) promised to patronize his real business with profit from the new business. Many of such victims feel that they're doing nothing wrong or that there was a hint of illegality when they complain of being scammed. In such cases, I only try to know, if the scammed business man is 100% sure that throughout the entire business that became a scam, there was never a time where *illegality,* which is not common in his normal daily business routine, was introduced! Many said no; there was never anything illegal but admitted that they sent blank company letterhead, invoice papers duly signed and stamped to their unknown business partners. Do you send blank company letterhead papers to your normal business customers? I normally ask. I simply deduce that it was at this stage that the offer was finally presented by their unknown business partners (scammers). The blank invoices were returned to him completed with inflated amount figure and the businessman still accepted to go ahead with the business. Apart from what the businessman stood to gain from the inflated amounts in the returned invoices, the business patronization promise was another offer. Actually a double offer was in this proposal and such offers are very common these days.

The offer is interpreted as the **promised gain** and is in every scammer's proposal, whether by email, phones, or physical contact. What is required from the scam target might be very negligible but there is always a gain if that negligible is done by the unsuspecting target no matter how you look at it.

Some local adages confirm so;

Every smoke starts with a fire.

Frogs do not run in the afternoon for nothing.

Different people read different meanings in a single common situation. People have different ways of perceiving gains. What you term as gain might mean nothing to the next person and vice versa. Some scammed victims will never accept they were pursuing a gain before they got scammed, but every victim of a scam had a motive facilitated by a promised gain that was to mature ultimately in that very business. Even in cases that the victim was requested to do something by the scammer that does not involve monetary expenses, there was something else that scammer promised the victim will gain or they will both gain.

There are situations one might not be willing to spend even a cent on a suspicious investment scheme but did the required registrations. Why? You registered because you stood to gain something by filling out the registration. I am unable to know exactly what you stood to gain, but the fact remains that some gain somewhere prompted you to fill out the registration. Even, if you were only seeking better information; *a sound mind knows that even the quest for better information is also a gain.* The resulting information if misleading is left for your judgment and can lead you into a scam.

A scam is never like a genuine business that you will invest to get a normal rate of profit return. In all scams, the promised gain is out of proportion compared to the projected input. All scams present a situation that you will only need to invest little or give a little assistance to gain a lot at maturity.

It is important to realize that most genuine businesses also have a projected gain for the business participants. The difference is that the projected gain in a scam business is a promise, actually an over blown promise from the scammer. The scammer, knowing that the business is a scam, will magnify the promised gain to entice the prospective victim into the business.

For any scam to be successful, the scam target or prospective victim must perceive the offer, or the promised gain in the scam proposal to be a worthy gain.

CHAPTER 17

COMPULSORY SALE OF CONFIDENCE

In all forms of scams, the scammers try to sell confidence. Sale of confidence is the scammer confiding privileged, rare information in the scam target. The scam proposal simply informs the scam target on a worthy secret unknown to many. If the scam target believes it, then he or she bought it. It is this bought confidence that the victim unconsciously tries to reciprocate later to the scammer and gets scammed. The initial giving of a very valuable thing to you for nothing is a sale of confidence. The valuable thing can be privileged information which can make you rich or improve your well-being.

Some scammers chasing your money sell privileged information that will make you rich while other scammers, chasing your private details, sell privileged information that will improve your well being. Example; a lottery scammer's proposal sells wealth while a phishing scammer purporting bank communication offers improvement in your bank account well being. Simply put, the scammer is confiding in you, that he has a privileged, rare opportunity to make money, or information that is advantageous.

Coming across an opportunity to make more money is the most common in modern scams being paraded. The idea is that the scam targets and victims are very lucky to have come across these wonderful opportunities. This first confidence in the scam target is always unique and plays a major role in making the target participate in the said transaction that might eventually be a scam. At the outset, eventual scam victims see themselves as blessed to have come across such opportunities and take advantage of such uncommon opportunities.

When an unknown woman pleads with you to keep a huge sum of money safely for her and promises to give you a good percentage for this service—she is simply selling a strong confidence to you. If you buy this confidence by participate in the business, it is possible that during the same business process of sending the money to you for keeps, she might plead with you to advance her some money to enable her to conclude a particular process in the same business to materialize your receiving the money for keeps. It will not be abnormal for you to reciprocate her earlier confidence in you by giving her the advance. Moreover, you stand to gain if the money arrives for keep. This is normal and common business practice if you trust the initial arrangement, unless you are informed otherwise. If you believed in the transaction, saw documentation and followed the whole process in details, believe me, you will not like to be the impediment in the promised gain coming to you.

Favors reciprocate favors—is the scammers' theory when setting up their targets and prospective victims.

Apart from those proposals where sale of confidence is very pronounced, sale of confidence is also present in HYIPs scams and other forms of scams, and should not be termed differently. The scam HYIP owner or conman simply offers rare opportunities for making easier money on websites or in advertisements as great opportunities, because not everyone are privileged to come across them. Even when an identity thief calls on phone to inform you that your bank account might be in danger and you should verify your personal details, the caller is simply selling confidence to you by informing you on something that might hurt your well-being. If you buy it, then you have released your personal details.

The prospective victim reciprocating an earlier confidence or taking advantage of a rare money making opportunity is actually what the scammer is chasing from day one. Make no mistakes about it; as long as you are a prospective victim in the scammer's business scheme, you stand a very good chance of reciprocating the earlier imparted confidence one day. Your reciprocation can also be in other ways than financial assistance.

Let us look at this situation;

A rough gem dealer was approached by chauffeur-driven Mr. Apia who wanted 1Kg of a particular size of unpolished garnet. Mr. Apia claimed he needed 1Kg from the gem dealer if he could supply the same sample size garnet as the one he showed. The gem dealer actually had some garnet which he showed Mr. Apia. Mr. Apia carefully chose 200g of his sample size. Sensing it might be his day, an opportunity to make more money, the gem dealer insisted that he will sell a gram of the chosen 200g for $25 each. The buyer,

Mr. Apia had no problems and simply paid the gem dealer $5,000 for the 200g. (What a day's profit for something that goes for $5 a gram). Before leaving, Mr. Apia now begged the gem dealer to assist him; that he still needed the balance 800g if the gem dealer could provide his sample size. Mr. Apia even promised he would make a large deposit for sourcing the further 800g of his sample size. Considering how nature favored his business that day, the gem dealer went searching immediately. After a long search, the only place the gem dealer could get the 800g was where they were selling the sample-size garnet for $50 a gram. Wise enough, the gem dealer first consulted Mr. Apia to inform him that his required size was very scarce and the going price was now $75 a gram. After normal business deliberations, Mr. Apia finally agreed to pay $75 a gram for the remaining 800g due to scarcity and urgency to conclude the purchase on his side. Upon concluding the deal with the gem dealer on the phone, Mr. Apia immediately drove to the gem dealers' shop and made a deposit of $5,000 for the incoming 800g. Now, the gem dealer only had to add $35,000, making $40,000, to buy the 800g at $50 from his secret seller, and then resell the gems to Mr. Apia at $75 a gram for a wonderful profit of $20,000. The gods must have remembered him that period. The gem dealer quickly used his money and bought the 800g consignment at $50 a gram. To date, the gem dealer is still waiting for Mr. Apia to come and pick up his 800g order or at least show up for his $5,000 deposit.

This whole arrangement was a set up. It was a 'scarcity scam' and the main purpose was to make the gem dealer pay $40,000 to a specific gem supplier (a sure colleague of Mr. Apia) buying garnet gem worth $4,000. The gem dealer ended up losing his money if a gram of garnet is still $5. He lost $30,000 and gained 800g of garnet worth $4,000 in the second transaction, so he lost heavily. Buying the initial 200g for an exorbitant $5,000 was the introductory sale of confidence. The later $5,000 deposit for 800g only insured the sale of confidence and the gem dealer bought it by entering into the deal. With the demonstration of confidence in the gem dealer, the gem dealer reciprocated by adding his personal money to make-up and buy the 800g Mr. Apia urgently needed at $50 per gram. He had already made some good profit from Mr. Apia and was to make even more profit from Mr. Apia after selling this new 800g to him at the agreed $75 new price.

In a con man's words;

'I sell confidence to people who repose same confidence in me and I betray theirs'. This is what scam or con is to be put simply.

The basis of all scams and cons is the sale of confidence and it comes in different selling forms; trust, kindness, gratitude, appeal, selection, luck, opportunity, etc. It is the same for all scams; gain to a privileged few who are opportune to come across. Likewise some of the new popular get-rich schemes on the internet via webinar, the presenter will tell you that you are among the first twenty-five or that this can only be done for the first twenty-five people: the art of selling confidence on offers. Now that you are among the first twenty-five people to come across this great opportunity to get rich in a world of about seven billion people, you may have to take advantage of this rare opportunity by going into the business!

Summarily, sale of confidence is in every scam, the form in which it is sold is what confuses many eventual scam victims. Scammers never hide that they are selling confidence, irrespective of the uniqueness of their proposed businesses (scam proposals), and their victims always buy these confidence. Scam victims are also unable to analyze or exactly explain when they bought these confidence the scammers were selling.

Always remember that, there is never the last of any business, opportunities revolve and there is nothing lucky in being the few selected for a suspicious business. You might simply be among the few selected to be scammed.

CHAPTER 18

A TARGETED COMMITMENT

In every successful scam, the scam victim was committed to that business. Targeted commitment was present in almost all successful scams. Targeted commitment is in the sense, that the victim had the commitment the scammer wanted in that very business. There are many types of commitment a prospective scam victim can demonstrate for an ongoing scam business venture, which may not tally with the kind of commitment the scammer seeks from the prospective victim. In Chapter 14 we discussed the different kinds of commitments a prospective victim can exhibit before becoming a scam victim. Unless the scammer achieves the desired kind of commitment in the prospective victim, the scam process is still in limbo and may not materialize as the scammer wishes.

A good example is the scammer doing everything possible to persuade the prospective victim to direct the business expenses to him or her. The scammer will want the prospective victim or victim to be comfortable with sending money to him or her directly for handling costs of doing business. The moment the victim starts feeling comfortable with this, then the scam has matured. Another is persuading the victim to always act promptly on anything that requires the victim's attention. The scammer also makes serious effort to achieve a targeted commitment level in the prospective victim's mind by mentioning time schedules, closing dates, and possible penalties for non timely compliance. All is in the bid of chasing the desired targeted commitment of the unsuspecting victim.

Targeted commitment is the commitment level where the scam victim now fully trusts the scammer in all ramifications. Thus, business expenses supposedly in the ensuing business transaction (scam) are sent to the scammer or paid through the scammer's directives. Whenever *ordinary commitment* and *business commitment* are fully established, the scammer will now plan on converting these commitments to targeted commitments, which involve making payments to the scammer directly or indirectly with the victim's trust, and satisfactory approval that such payments as business expenses will be used judiciously as expected or rather as suggested by the scammer in achieving their joint goal.

As earlier discussed, for instance, the scammer can tell the victim that it is cheaper to hire a lawyer to represent him or her when signing agreement documents than traveling to sign the documents personally. If this is a scam and the scammer scheme involves the signing of agreement documents, then the scammer is only trying to get the victim to send the money allocated for traveling to him or her. The scammer can also tell the victim that he or she will be able to raise part of the present business expense to be made; the scammer is only trying to know exactly when the victim has his or her own part of the contribution to re-direct This is the targeted commitment from the victim which the scammer has been chasing from the onset.—That full trust that their joint interest will be covered by either party.

As earlier said too, there is no business in a scam business and nothing is real, so the scammer must be careful before the unsuspecting victim wastes money that the scammer is chasing elsewhere, thinking the business is real. This is one of the **unknown transactions** the scammer is busy trying to accomplish frequently, that prospective victims do not know.

The scam victim, trusting the scammer with a cent, is better for the scammer and the scam scheme, than the unsuspecting victim paying the airline or any other entity thousands. Situations like this create further trust and hopefully there will be more stories from the scammer for more business expenses in the future as the scam progresses. This is the most important and the targeted commitment from the prospective victim the scammer wants.

In a majority of scam cases reported, I have observed that a target committed scam victim simply sees all expenses as business expenses, so it does not matter to that scam victim who the payment is made to as long as the purpose of making such payment is fulfilled with satisfaction. At this stage of commitment from the victim, the scammer's directives will become very powerful and the former prospective scam victim will now become a scam victim. In the same fashion, scam victims become actual scam victims.

Most scam businesses where the prospective victims are business committed are easier to progress to targeted commitments as long, as the prospective victim understands that there are costs for doing business, which are also applicable in genuine businesses.

There are also cases, where the ordinary commitments lead directly to targeted commitments without involving any business commitment process. These types of scams are most common on the Internet. Normally these Internet scams have websites that explain every business step (business process) of the proposed venture. The moment you show interest, you get ordinarily committed by filling out the registration forms and afterwards make payments to the scammer directly (targeted commitment). It is unlike the other types of scams where the scammer must wait for the prospective victim's response to being able to decide on his or her best extorting method, for everybody is unique in nature. Going from ordinary commitment to targeted commitment is also common in scam adverts. The advertisements have already explained the whole business process, so there is no need for a business commitment from the victim.

In some other cases, business commitment and targeted commitment are woven into one, particularly in high-paying scams. There are scams that have business processes and require business commitment such as the money transfer scams, wash money scams, the bequest (inheritance) scams, lottery scams, etc. In these kinds of scams, there are conventional business processes that must be followed for the prospective victim to understand why there are business costs and expenses before the promised gain in the scam proposal can materialize. The scammer proves these business processes to the victim with documents and papers. The main feature here is that, similar genuine business processes are being imitated, so a business process must ensue to the clarity of the prospective victim before that prospective victim can participate in the business expenses. Also, in such cases, the scammer must wait for the business commitment from the prospective victim to convert into a targeted commitment. Any indiscriminate request for the victim's business expense, as business cost can jeopardize the whole scam.

Business commitments can suddenly become targeted commitments in some scams. Scams with such characteristics are the cheque scam, the ATM card scam, etc. In these scams, there is business commitment as the prospective victim is already using the cheque or ATM card as instructed by the scammer. The prospective victim might have submitted the cheque for clearing or has withdrawn money from the ATM card, and then suddenly the business process of withdrawing more money or the cheque clearing is stopped or cut short unless a withholding clause is rectified. Rectification of such clause is normally a finale payment to be made by the victim. The business commitment here is the victim accepting the normal process of withdrawing with the ATM card or paying the cheque into his or her bank. When the victim has done this part, the targeted commitment now comes in; the victim is asked to help rectify the clause withholding further ATM card withdrawals or the bank cheque clearing. The scammer achieving targeted commitment in these peculiar scams is often easy because the unsuspecting victim is like a live-witness of the business processes.

Ordinary commitment was present in all successful scams. Business commitment might or might not have been present in all successful scams, depending on the scammer's scheme or the business process of the scam, but targeted commitment was present in all successful scams.

Whenever one is getting too committed to a business, there is need for a recheck of that whole business process from the origin. Recheck from how it all started. As I mentioned earlier, **commitment is what does the damage to the scam victims in any scam business**. It is the commitment that hurt and played the psychological role in making those victims lose their money to the scams and scammers

CHAPTER 19

COMPULSORY ADVANCE PAYMENT

In every successful scam, the victim made an advance payment. The main stock in trade of scammers is luring a victim into making an advance payment for a want, or release private information for a desire. The victim has been scammed because he or she has paid for something that did not materialize. The victim has been scammed because he or she has been lured into making business expenses in a nonexistent business transaction. To make an advance payment or release private information prior to an expected final outcome, are all that the scammer is busy convincing the prospective victim to do. Therefore we can say that in all scam, the scammer is either trying to lure you into providing your private information for something you want or to use later, or trying to lure you into making an advance payment for one thing or another. Scammers achieve these intentions in very different sophisticated ways naming them anything suitable. But the primary object of the whole plan is to extort something upfront. Scammers simple elicit an action from you in advance.

If a person can prevent making an advance payment on anything whatsoever, then it might be difficult to scam such a person.

The mere observation of an advance payment request in an unknown business transaction is enough to create great suspicion of scam until proven otherwise. This is serious and should be treated as such. Anyone avoiding scams should treat all upfront payment requests from business partners as scams, until all parties concerned prove beyond reasonable doubt that they are genuine. Compulsorily, there was advance payment in those scams where the scam victims made payments to the scammers or to the scammer's directives, no matter how they are interpreted.

If there was no promised gain, there would not have been any advance payment for it. It is clear that victims make these advance payments on arising business success snags in the business, hoping to recoup them later when the promised gain materializes.

The scammer can plot an advance payment to be hidden or open. The same scammer can plot the whole scam scheme to persuade the present victim into luring another person to make an advance payment. Advance payment can be much disguised, but it is present in most victim payment scams. Advance payment can be hidden or open, depending on the scammer's scheme of obtaining this advance payment from the unsuspecting victim.

Scammers elicit an advance action or payment is another confusing aspect to understanding scams. What exactly the victim was paying for is confusing in the sense that each individual is different in what he or she can pay for. Some can pay for even happiness, while others cannot pay for such. What the scammer tries to do is to use any conviction possible, any method available, any means within reach to lure the unsuspecting victim into believing a business transaction is real and worth making business expenses for. Many people are very willing to spend huge money in advance for them to be appointed as ambassadors. Others are willing to spend anything upfront to get a job at the United Nations. In some cases, what the victim expects to get in making the advance payment or action might be far less than what has already been spent or done. Our individual perception of what is at stake differs. Different people value the same thing differently.

Mr. Noah lost $500,000 to scammers, trying to become a federal minister in his country.

Constitutionally, in his country, Mr. Noah could only be a minister for 4 years maximum even if he was appointed. The salary of a minister in Mr. Noah's country is about $5,000 a month. So, in 4 years, he could not have officially earned more than $240,000. Mr. Noah, as you can see, has invested more than he was expecting to gain. I quite agree that there are other attributes that go with being a minister he might have been interested in but this same offer can be rejected by another person who is not willing to spend $500,000 in the one go, for a salary of $240,000 in 4 years. Individuals vary and their priorities vary. Likewise, one man's meat can be another man's poison. Scammers also exploit these individual variations in eliciting advance payments and actions.

Advance payments when called different names such as; registration fee, activation fee, online auction bid units, government taxes, attorney fees, remittance fee, processing fees, affidavit fee, etc., are not easy to detect as advance payments as scammers call them. The fact is that the victim is being made to release some money upfront before whatever the victim is expecting comes through. No matter how the scam scheme or plan was set, in any scam, where the scam victim made payments to the scammer before conclusion of the business, were advance payments. Even in cases where the scamming did not work, believe me, the scam scheme or plan had an advance payment request scheduled, which the scammer didn't have the opportunity to present to his or her prospective victim.

Every scam victim that made payments to the scammer was lured into believing that, whatever was to be gained in the business was worth making advance payment.

Literally, when scam victims report being scammed to the police, they are actually complaining that something they paid for or for which they made a deposit, was eventually not provided to them. Even if the victim had been planning to donate the promised gain to charity, whatever the good intention was, it must have been worth something, that spending money ('the lost money') upfront was comfortable for that victim. If the intention was ultimately not realized, and the money was not refunded, the victim will surely complain because, he or she has paid for a particular service to fulfill an intention, which did not materialize. Many scam victims misunderstand what they should be complaining about. They hardly present the right claim. We will discuss some right claims in Chapter 27 Part 4.

Advance payment can also be hidden making it difficult to detect, such situations are very common in internet scams. The scammer in this case tries to use websites to explain all that the unsuspecting victim will need to know or will ever need to ask about the business. Buying the bid units of an online auction scam is a hidden advance payment. The bought bid units will remain with you until you use them to bid for something you might never win or does not exist.

When one loses money in a HYIP scam, one simply made an advance payment, expecting the promised investment return which never materialized, so you were scammed. For instance, even if a scam HYIP paid the initial two investments before vanishing on the third investment, it is still a case of advance payment, since you are still waiting for the third investment returns for which you have already made advance payments.

If the business you were doing was genuine and not hidden in secrecy, there are letters of credit, bank guarantees and post dated checks which are legal tenders and commitments that stand in courts, so why make quick advance payments to anyone? I repeat that if you can prevent an advance payment on anything whatsoever then it might be difficult to scam you. The irony is that most things that are genuine do not run on advance payment; you normally pay after the service has been rendered.

Advance payment requests must come from the scammer in any scam and they appear as finale payment requests bearing suitable names. Those business costs paid upfront while waiting for the promised gain to materialize are advance payments.

Payment made by the victim to the scammer or through the scammer's directives in a scam business is an advance payment, for the promised gain of the business.

CHAPTER 20

SYSTEMATIC BILLING AND SELF BILLINGS IN SCAM BUSINESS

Systematic Billing is a common feature in scams. Scammers employ tactics in making payment requests to their unsuspecting victims. The majority of payments made by the scam victim in most scam business were systematically requested by the scammer. Systematic billing is very common in scams that involve business processes. The only deviations to these are found in 'hit and run' scams where the scammers expect only one main payment from their victims.

Normally, in most scam business processes I have analyzed, the prospective victim starts by making smaller payments to the scammer, which gradually increase as the victims gets more committed in the scam business. I have also noticed that the scammer's payment requested amount does not always increase; sometimes it decreases.

I often wondered how victims end up paying such a large sum of money to a scammer. My analyses show that scammers systematically adjust payment requests to be logical to that scam victim. The scammer makes payment requests smaller or bigger each time with good reason.

In several scam victims' interviews, their scammers never tried making these payment requests sums progressive or incremental. Instead they employed a tactical or systematic billing system that in itself makes the next payment less than the total past payment and logical to the victim. Every new payment requested is very logical in relation to the past payments same victim has made. The scammer's art in systematic billing simply controls the psychological reasoning of the victim; is making this new payment advantageous than losing all past payments? Is losing all previous business inputs better than making this new payment? These are the ultimate questions posed to the victim through systematic billing. Gradually, the total payments made by the victim become a huge sum and converts into a deep commitment that was not planned in most cases.

If you have already spent $1,000 in a business venture, will spending another $300 deprive you of the success of that business? Also, after spending the additional $300, will an additional and apparently crucial $650 make you forget the $1,300 already spent in total so far?

Systematic billing is very common and one of the main reasons why scam victims lost large sums of money in scam businesses. A scam starts with little expenses which gradually become big payments accumulatively. Every new payment request from the scammer to the victim is very logical and small when compared to the total already spent by the victim in that business.

Most paying scam victims just cannot forget the business due to their past expenses in the business. Example; a scam business worth millions of dollars can have an attorney who will accept a $500 attorney fees payment. The $500 payments might be small but it will play a big part in committing the victim further into that very business. Later on, the same attorney might start demanding $3,000 with vigor because the same victim has previously paid $500 eight times. Systematic billing is very effective in scams. It reaches a stage, whereby the scam victim does not pay, means, he or she does not have the money or cannot raise it from any possible source.

Scam victims need to understand that every payment to the scammer is a profit for him or her, and demonstrates a further commitment on the part of the victim, whether it was $10 or $10,000. As long as the prospective victim or victim keeps paying finale payment requests, the extortion scheme is in progress, which is what matters to the scammer since he or she set-up the scam to make more money. If you have already invested $10,000 in a business, you will not allow an additional $800 to deprive you of the investment reward, so you will make the additional $800 payment. In a bid to prevent the loss of $10,000, you now have a total of $10,800 to prevent losing. To the victim's reasoning; making this next (always last) payment is better than losing the total previous expenses by allowing the business to go bankrupt.

Scam business are fictitious business made to look real and they have no conclusion except promises, so the majority of scammers hang onto these systematic billings, quoting one business success snag or another, gradually extorting money from their victims, while ensuring that no new payment request exceeds the total past payments, until those victims bill themselves *(self billing)*. Systematic billing can last for months and years, resulting in huge scam losses that many people wonder how the victim could have paid such large amount to the scammer.

Self billing is characteristic of fully developed scams. This is when the scam victims impose further expenses (extortions) on themselves unknowingly. This is common in scams and borne mostly out of the victim's anxiety to finalize the business, he or she does not know is a scam. The scammer knows self billing will manifest as the scamming progresses and patiently waits for it. Attracting a finale payment requests from the scammers is very common in victims whose patience have been thoroughly stretched by the frustrating business venture. I term it to be self billing because this finale payment request would not have emanated, if the victim did not create the situation that prompted the scammer to make the request.

When the prospective victim has invested so much money or even committed so much to a business he or she does not know is a scam, it is common that anxiety as to when the business will end will manifest. Such a victim might ask his or her business partner what actually is delaying the conclusion of their business. Without the knowledge that the business is a scam, he or she has just provided an avenue for the scammer to claim that anything is responsible for the non-conclusion of the business, which will appear as business expenditure.

My observations in most successful scams, showed that, most scammers will hang unto systematic billing, waiting for that victim's anxiety in order to ask for a major finale payment. Self billing is a sure test to know if any lingering business transaction is a scam. Simply ask your business partner in the lingering business what it will take to finalize the business. If your business partner insists that a final monetary input is needed for the conclusion of the business, then you might be in a scam business.

It is also possible that a well committed prospective victim who has not paid the scammer even a cent might ask the unknown business partner 'what will conclude this whole business'—self billing. Likewise, a victim already paying the scammer systematically might be so worried after several payments without anything to show for them, that he or she wants to know 'what will finally conclude this whole, long business'—self billing. When a prospective scam victim or scam victim asks such questions, he or she has offered the scammer a finale payment request opportunity. If the prospective scam victim has never paid the scammer before, then the scammer will present a finale payment request. If, on the other hand, the scam victim has been paying the scammer before, then the scammer will raise the finale payment request amount. I have repeatedly observed that self billing is a great opportunity for the scammer. It might work or not but it is a great opportunity to define the scam.

I once asked a scam victim why he suddenly decided to deviate from the normal $200 or $300 payments to his unknown business partner, and paid $7,000 at once upon expressing his suspicion. He said his business partner said that $7,000 will conclude the business. Also, he wanted the business to conclude more rapidly after spending over six months of his time waiting and seeing no result. Moreover, he said that he had been transferred to their office in Beijing. He did not want to continue with the calls, faxes and discussions about this same business, from their Beijing office. He actually wanted a fresh start there—with the promised gain.

I observed that it is because of the systematic billing and self billing which will follow in the scamming process, that the scammer desperately wants the prospective victim to commit financially to the business. The scammer will do whatever is possible to make a prospective victim issue the first payment which is the most important. In scams, the victim's first payment is relative in setting the systematic billings of the victim, which in turn must lead to self billing unless the victim discovers the scam nature of the business. Scammers have generally modified discharge payments to accommodate and induce early victim commitment.

Systematic billing and self billing in most scams businesses, work hand in hand, each can lead to the other, and they also worked side by side in very huge successful scams.

A Lebanese business man, after spending over $700,000 in a scam business, was so worried that he asked his business partners

'what will make this business conclude finally'. He just wanted to resolve the whole problem once and for all to receive his expected gain of $42,000,000 payment. His business partners told him that the only problem delaying his payment was the non payment of a certain compulsory government fee. The Lebanese business man asked how much was this compulsory government fee. The scammers replied it was a 2.5% fee and unavoidable. Considering past expenses ($700,000), future profits to be made and the need to finalize this business and face other things possibly, the Lebanese business man made the $1,050,000 payment. The whole business was a scam.

You will notice that the Lebanese business man indirectly set up the 2.5% bill. Most scammers use mere systematic billings to keep their victims in line, waiting for their victims' anxiety to develop into self billing. The scammers above might have been requesting several sums from the Lebanese man systematically, claiming it was for this and that expenses to release their $42,000,000 (promised gain); bribe, stamp, attorney fees, processing fees, etc. The Lebanese man must have been paying them for him to spend $700,000 but when he decided it was too much and taking too long, he ended up billing himself indirectly and making his total loss now $1,750,000 to the scammers. Now, he has to chase a total of $1,750,000 already spent—deep commitment. You will also notice here that self billing can make the scammer increase the finale payment request amount. This is so because self billing is equivalent to the scam victim's wish; business over or conclude business and get promised gain—decide?

Another good example is the internet scam schemes.

Normally you will only be required to get your first website for say $9.45. After which a website in your name will be made available as yours. The traffic to your own website will be almost zero. You are forced to ask the 'designers' how traffic to your website can be increased to generate the promised/expected income. The software that will increase your website traffic costs $145.00 and you are 'properly' advised to get additional 24 better designed websites to generate the earlier advertised and promised income stream, etc. In short 'why not take advantage of our reduced full package price offer which is only $199.95 if you pay now, to receive 25 websites, guaranteed traffic plus income streamer, plus 24hr special customer service'.

The story above is a typical example that is very common on the internet these days and many are getting scammed daily on the above proposal. You will notice here that what the prospective victim saw as a mere $9.45 expense is gradually turning into a $200.00 or more expense. Even after you buy the discounted full package offer for $199.95, there will still be another last thing to keep the anticipated income streaming, probably the $69 'robot earner' that will generate continuous income even when you are on holidays. If you have paid to this stage, I wonder how you will let $209.40 go to waste rather than spend a mere $69 for the robot earner, so you buy the robot earner, simple. This is a clear example of systematic billing. Any question the investor asks, can lead to a major expenses (self billing).

The force driving the victims in such scams is not only the initial meager amount spent but the business processes of such scams. The processes involve serious commitment from the victim geared toward the ultimate desire to succeed. Such scam websites never miss detailed explanations, gradual investment stages, beautiful graphics, video interviews, success stories, etc., all well designed to make the victim's desire for success larger and the chase more exhilarating. The majority of such investment schemes are scams; one thing leads to another and another leads to yet another. This is the way of scam businesses; you keep chasing your past expenses and in that process you incur more expenses to chase yet again. It just goes on and on.

There was a case study, where the scammers allowed the victim to get some profit in the business before the promised gain matured. I understood on further inquiry that it was for further commitment of the victim. This action has a disarming effect on almost a 100% of paying scam victims. As a matter of fact, whenever some 'perceived' good results (gain) materializes in a scam business, the scammer did it purposely to keep the victim or prospective victim in line or lure the victim into larger commitments. This is seen in some scam HYIPs that might allow their prospective victim to escape with $3 interest paid on a $10 investment. The reason is to lure the investor (victim) into larger investments.

Victims who perceived some gains must realize that, there is never a time in a scam business or will there ever be a time that the materializing good result (gain) for the victim will exceeds that victim's past expense in that scam business. This is a constant you will notice in such scam stories.

Mr. Gorge, after spending over $480,000, was happy that his payment was finally coming to him via cash payment in his native country. He prepared for the day, bought a big trunk box and visited the finance company in Central Budapest. He was well received by the financial firm agents. After due identification and Mr. Gorge's payment of another $4,000 demurrage fees to the finance firm, the cash money cleaning process finally started. Mr. Gorge had previously been told by the scammers that the cash was coded to reduce suspicion by authorities while in transit which was okay with him. When the cleaning process started, the chemists could only clean $13,000 before problems developed; more cleaned cash started turning out in bad color after cleaning. The chemist insisted that he needed reacting powders and without the necessary powders; the entire cash might be ruined. So they needed a reacting powder costing about $500,000. The scammers left Mr. Gorge to go with the already cleaned $13,000. Two weeks later, Mr. Gorge paid the $500,000 and the story continued as anti-terrorist authorities moved in, and so on. It was just another scam.

You will notice that when Mr. Gorge left with the $13,000—the fact had a lot of psychological effect on him. Surely, he must have checked elsewhere, if the cleaned $13,000 currencies were genuine, which he confirmed. Also, $13,000 is some big money to leave with Mr. Gorge, confirming that the financial agents could be trusted. All these considerations induced him into paying the $500,000 for the reacting powder.

There was only one thing Mr. Gorge did not consider—the $13,000 he had was still his money, having spent altogether $480,000 plus $4,000 on that fateful day. Unfortunately, Mr. Gorge considered only the present $4,000 he paid and got $13,000 on the same day. This is what happens in some scams, and where the effectiveness of scam networks discussed in Chapter 24, comes in.

Whenever the materializing good result in a confirmed scam business exceeds the victim's past expenses in monetary value, then the scammer miscalculated or was taken unawares by the prospective victim. The scammer misjudged the prospective victim's greed or totally misunderstood the scam victim's surroundings.

I once invested $80 in a HYIP, after 4 days I was paid $100 as promised (25% gain). I then added another $20 making my total investments $120 and after 4 days, again I was paid $150. I withdrew my whole money (principals plus interests) without investing a further penny in that HYIP.

For a full month on a daily basis, that very HYIP was sending me emails and messages soliciting my further investments. They even wrote a special letter advertising a special 200% 3 days investment reward for only past investors like me. It was all re-scheduling which is characteristic of scam and to make me reinvest because my exit was not anticipated then. Maybe, they expected me to increase my investments or they miscalculated their projection of my actions. The truth is that I was doing a minor research then, theirs was the first suspicious HYIP from that part of Europe and I wanted to know what they were up to.

It is also possible that the person who introduced my email to the scammers assured them a minimum of $500 investment from me. They might have been waiting for the 'hit' (bigger investment) which never came. Meanwhile, their $50 is still in my account. Simply put, I was lucky, months later I learnt that a friend of mine in London lost £600 to the same HYIP that paid me $50 as profit. My friend started with £100, was paid £125 (25% profit) after 4 days, he put in another £500 investment and lost all £625. Funny, I am sure if I had invested more, I would have lost all. The only truth I could have told my friend to prevent him being scammed, if I had the opportunity, was that *'25% profit in a business investment after 4 days is not possible, even. If it was possible, the HYIP will not share it that easily'.* If he believed me, then I might have saved someone from being scammed. Even, telling him to make a small investment such as I did could also be disastrous, because every scam business is unique in its premises—he might not behave exactly like me. In the right reasoning, if the HYIP is so sure of their system, many banks would be willing to loan them money for their business.

The Internet has one of the greatest conducive environment for playing systematic billings and self billings. Everyone wants easy money, so, using systematic and self billings; so many scams are now on the Internet. A majority of us find it difficult to understand that it is difficult for anyone or any business arrangement to teach another how to become rich for a fee. One can only be taught how to make a living but no one can teach another directly how to become a millionaire or become the next wealthy person. Anyone becoming the next billionaire after learning how to make a living is entirely left to that person's hard work, knowledge and the present success opportunities available. No one can teach another how to become a very rich person in a regular business except in an irregular business.

Imagine the number of **get-rich, high income earning and high yield investment programs** on the Internet and you will know how many people are involved in scams. How to make money and become the next richest man is a secret which wealthy people guard desperately against any intrusive or curious inquisitor. Even the richest men and women in the world cannot market to anyone how to become a millionaire. It is impossible to market their know-how, for a fee as seen all over the internet. A successful person can only show another a means of livelihood. He or she cannot even guarantee that the same system will succeed for that person. But the majority of 'get rich quick' schemes around seem to guarantee definite success in becoming a millionaire like 'them'. These schemes are well prepared that all you end up achieving is making the presenter richer while hoping for your good fortune.

There are laws that prevent workers from exposing company secrets, prototypes, knowledge, etc. Known successful CEOs guard their business knowledge. There are laws protecting ownerships of various endeavors. Humans are greedy by nature and love dominating the world. A successful process is normally a secret to that successful person.

Somehow, *I believe that legitimate profit making (genuine business) is not 'distributed'. It is guarded, protected and possibly monopolized. It is irregular profit making (scam business) that tends to be shared, unguarded and broadcasted, creating room for more scams.*

CHAPTER 21

RE-APPEARING FINALE PAYMENTS

It is straight forward that finale payments must manifest in all scams. Finale payment is the payment made by the scam victim in a scam business that will resolve a business success snag for the promised gain of the business to materialize. Finale payments in scams are normally paid to the scammer or directed by the scammer. The scammer having made the nonexistent business (scam) appear existent to the unsuspecting victim will now employ finale payment requests as the means of extracting money from the victim.

Scammers will tactically ensure that all business processes in the business leads to a snag or hitch, which only monetary input can resolve, so that the scammer will call upon the victim to help remove the business success snag or hitch. Finale payments benefit the scammer and are the scammer's original plan of getting the victim's monies. It is the scammer's grand design of extorting the victim.

All scam businesses are schemed for finale payments and several finale payments appear in scam businesses.

Finale payments appear in many forms but they are supposed to remove one problem or the other that will conclude the business. A victim involved in a scam business process as presented by the scammer, might not easily understand these genuine-looking finale payment requests, because, the scammer imitates the processes of another similar genuine business, but now implants business success snags throughout the processes to enable finale payment requests to the victim.

Tactfully, the scammer will make finale payment requests to appear as problems for all participants in the business to solve. However, the scammer will look to the prospective victim to solve the problem, as a demonstration of gratitude for being part of the business. Remember; the privileged information and the great opportunity presented to the victim, plus being amongst the very few selected or the only person selected, is enough to warrant some gratitude in return. For instance, in a money transfer scam, the victim is privileged to be selected, has been given a great opportunity to become very rich and has been trusted to keep custody of the whole money; which is enough for the victim to show some gratitude. At least show gratitude by assisting in removing a business success snag or hitch that will enable all the above mentioned gains to materialize.

Finale payments are also those payments by the victim in a scam that will progress the business to a conclusion stage. They are also that last lump sum investment that will earn handsomely in an investment scam scheme ultimately. Finale payments also include; that last tip (bribe) that will make customs officials look the other way for the consignment to cross the border, that last investment that will resolve all complications, the cost of that last software that will make the desired traffic flow and the monies roll in, the cost of that last website that will generate the desired income, the cost of that special robot that will predict forex movement, that last payment to the topmost authority that will release your payment, etc. They are all finale payment made by the victim if that business is a scam. Finale payment requests are the scammers' main show; always that last business cost or last expenses for everything to materialize. In every scam, finale payments and their requests will appear and re-appear, they keep appearing forever, because there is no business conclusion in a scam business, until the scam victim realizes the business is a scam

The scammer makes finale payments appear as pavers for the awaited financial freedom. Whenever the scammer requests a finale payment from the victim, it will showcase as the long awaited solution to everything in the business. Then the finale payment will appear again as a different solution to another problem that was not envisaged during the last finale payment, then it will appear yet again, and so on.

Finale payments are difficult for scam victims to detect because each new finale payment request bears a different name and arises from a different situation. Finale payments and their requests can assume any name the scammer wishes; it can be a manufactured name that suits the ongoing business and can also be an imported name from a similar genuine business process.

A good example is the scammer telling the prospective victim in a lottery scam that before he or she is paid lottery winnings, the government insists that all lottery winners must pay '**export tax**'. Export tax is an official tax of several governments worldwide but it is not applicable here. The lottery winner (victim) is not exporting anything, but expecting a payment. The suitability of the word 'export tax' from another view can also seem right to this victim in this ongoing lottery scam. After all, there is money to be paid outside the country of the lottery organizer which can be termed as export. Finale payments and their requests are confusing and convincing to most scam victims.

The purest characteristic of scam is the continuous manifestations of finale payments; the constant re-appearance of one last expense that will materialize the promised gain.

The scammer can request this last expense (finale payment) or make it manifest through the business processes or documentations in the business. The scammer in every scam business will continue to present finale payment for the victim to pay, assist in paying, solve or assist in solving the problems until the victim bill himself or herself, or detects the whole business is a scam. Even after self billing and payment by the scam victim, finale payments will start to reappear again if the scam victim is still keen on achieving success in the business. These are the only possible actions of the scammer; because, the business is a scam, and can never materialize to whatever the victim is hoping. Victims in scam businesses will continue paying finale payment requests through systematic billing or self billing until they're broke financially. If the commitment to succeed in the business is still highly present but the victim is out financially, the scammer can transform the whole transaction into occultism. We will discuss the aspect of *scam occultism* in chapter 23.

Systematic billing is applied in finale payment requests by the scammer. Once the scam has matured, the scammer sticks to systematic billings and will introduce self billing as the scam victim prompts it.

If the business is a scam, examples of some finale payment requests are;

'**Everything will start working well if you buy the $299 full package**'.

'**The only thing withholding your payment is your non payment of the 0.2% government tax**'.

'If you pay the $25,000 wire charges, the money will be in your account within 48 hours'.

'Why not buy our $1,500 full package, which is fully automated in income generation?'

'The contract is yours but we need $2,000 to register your company officially'.

'To wire your lottery winnings by TT will cost you $1,800 wire charges'.

'The cheaper $500,000 reacting powder is all we need now to clean the whole money with no further problems'.

'To appoint an attorney will cost $5,000 to sign for the immediate award of the contract'.

It goes on and on. You will notice that each request looks conclusive, and supposedly, the next step after paying the requested amount will be materialization of the promised gain or business conclusion, but it will never be. In scams, another problem requiring another finale payment must emerge afterwards. This process will continue until that victim is wise enough to know it is a scam or financially out.

If you detect finale payment requests in a business transaction, then that business transaction is definitely a scam. You will not get whatever you are hoping for by paying the finale payment requests. Even, if the finale payment requests are coming for someone you trust, maybe that person you trust is not aware of what he or she is being used for.

The reason the scammer gives, for the last expense that will resolve everything (finale payment), is always very logical to the scam victim but no finale payment is the last. Another problem with another logical reason to be solved will reappear again, and another finale payment to be made.

The extortions in scam businesses are all about finale payment requests and compliance.

CHAPTER 22

FREQUENT DEADLINES RESCHEDULING

Changes in deadlines and rescheduling of deadlines are common and characteristic of scam businesses. The scammer reschedules deadlines and makes changes to the maturity dates for concluding the business or stages of the business frequently. The scammer's main objective is to get the victim's money, so as long as the scammer's objectives are not being accomplished accordingly, the scammer will have to make adjustments to the business processes to accommodate the main objective of the whole business, which is monetary extortion of the victim.

Scammers postpone and reschedule deadlines in scam businesses to;

A. Accommodate unforeseen difficulties in the victim's finance:

The scam victim might actually be having difficulties in raising money to make the finale payments as directed by the scammer, so the scammer has to change the deadline because what the scammer wants is the victim's payments and cannot tell the victim that the business deadline has expired. The scammer, therefore, has to reschedule deadlines for the victim to raise money and make payments, since obtaining payments from the scammer, is the primary objective of the whole scheme.

B. Assess the victim's faith and keep the victim's hope alive.

Scammers use deadlines to check the victim's determination to succeed and the commitment level of the victim. The business (scam) is supposed to be over if the almighty deadline is not met in time, which is not the scammer's desire. To the scammer, a committed victim should be bothered with deadlines unless that victim does not want the business to succeed. The creation of a deadline can make a victim buckle down and buckle to the business.

C. Create room for further maneuvering of the victim

Even when the victim has done all that is expected according to scammer's directives, the scammer still has to postpone the date of materialization of the promised gain because, in reality, there is no business being done and no gain will materialize anytime soon. Scams are like hoaxes; acts, make-beliefs, and the storylines will never make them real no matter what.

It is common for the person (scammer) to say *'this will be impossible to get again if it is not paid by the 18th of August', and do not be surprised if the same person (scammer) calls again on the 28th of August or even 2 months later to ask if you have raised the money.* It is common in scam businesses, to run a supposedly one week business for one year or more. The ever extending duration of a scam business is made possible due to frequent deadline rescheduling.

A scam victim's capabilities are unknown and infinite, so the scammer cannot put a true deadline. Also, the scammer cannot set a limit in the financial capabilities of a victim when the scammer's sole purpose is extorting as much as possible from the scam victim. I have observed that scammers never believe their victims can reach their peak of financial extortion, so they open the possibility for further extortion by rescheduling deadlines.

An aberration to postponing deadlines is only possible when the scammer knows the victim very well, and **wants to end the whole scam without suspicion from the victim or wants to impose blame on the victim.** This is very possible in trust scams that originated from physical person to person contact. The unknown scammer in this case can assess the whole scam scheme and victim physically; knowing when to quit or continue, knowing when the victim has money or not and even knowing when the victim has reported the scam to the police authorities. The knowledge and victim's details available to the scammer in such physical contact trust scams make it very dangerous to victims and also very difficult to unravel. Scams set this way have completely ruined very rich people and still cannot be unraveled.

Moreover, a scam victim might, out of anxiety, fix a deadline to stop investing further in the frustrating business, if it fails to conclude by then. In a scam, this action will only result in a finale payment request (self billing) from the scammer to meet such victim's imposed deadline.

Mr. Welles informed his partner that he will cease further expenses in the business if the business did not conclude by December 1990. His partners (scammers) informed him that everything was okay except for the transfer charges to send the money to him. So, Mr. Welles sent $340,000, being 1% wire charges, to them to enable them pay the wire charges and transfer his $34,000,000.

It was a scam, so, Mr. Welles imposed the deadline (perceived as self billing by the scammer) that led to a finale payment request that cost Mr. Welles $340,000. The self billing here was also caused by the victim's anxiety to conclude the fictitious business. The main motive driving Mr. Welles was his imagination to earn $34,000,000. If there was ever $34,000,000 to transfer to him, he did not have to pay wire charges, which could have been deducted from the source. This is also a good example of imagination blocking realization. *(Imagination and realization struggle Chapter 25)*

Investigations into deadline shifts in genuine businesses also showed a pattern; those genuine companies were either, telling lies in their service claims or they were making customers pay more than the value of their products or services with these deadline shifts. I can affirm that even businesses perceived as genuine, with continuous deadline rescheduling are scam related. One just has to investigate exactly what that genuine business is scamming.

A genuine estate development firm was collecting $200 monthly from 2000 land subscriber to which they will allocate plots of land in a new estate. The estate development firm kept postponing the land allocation date for over two years only to refund each subscriber their $4800 deposit. All refunded subscribers were happy to get $4800 refund on this definite scam.—The estate development firm had $9,600,000 investment power unaccounted for.

Summarily, if a business has so many deadlines and these deadlines are easily shifted for one reason or the other, then a full blown scam might be in progress. ***Remember that the deadlines in a scam business are rescheduled forever because there was no business in the first instance and it follows that such a fictitious business could not have a date of maturity.*** Just like the genuine estate development firm above, that had no land to allocate to any subscriber.

CHAPTER 23

SCAM OCCULTISM AND THE SECRECY

The most common manifestation of occultism in scams, the majority of us will understand easily, is in the so called confidentiality treaties seen in most scam businesses. These confidentiality treaties are normally adhered to by scam victims in scam businesses. Scammers easily convince their victims to keep their business secret, and also some victim, decide on their own to keep the whole business a secret. Confidentiality request is present in all major scams and should be properly understood if one is to avoid scams. It is evidently clear, that many scam victims were religious in their approach to the business that scammed them. Such victims believed in one thing or the other, they might have even over believed in themselves. Certain supernaturalisms appear in scams to the disbelief of many, but are yet common in advanced scam business situations.

In scam occultism, the scammer has now introduced supernatural phenomena into the scamming process or there is belief in supernatural forces in the ensuing business transaction (scam). Many scam victims that lost huge sums of money were under the spell of this occultism if they would honestly tell their stories in full details. I can also say that such victims were in a cultic arrangement of which they were not aware. This supernatural phenomenon in most cases is introduced directly or indirectly by the scammers but believed by their scam victims. There are also situations where the victim, due to background, will introduce the supernatural phenomenon.

People's beliefs should not be underestimated by any standard. In the eastern world it is very common for businesspersons to imbibe their religions into their daily business life, unlike in the western world, where most people see religion as a Sunday going affair. Superstition is irrational and deep seated in most occurrences. In superstitious beliefs, there are convictions that the performing or non-performing of certain actions brings good or bad luck, and that some happenings are spiritual. This sort of strong belief in the supernatural or spiritual dimension to events can be one strong driving force in some business ventures. If a business with one participant of such belief is a scam (a scam business with a scam victim of such belief), then a scammer's paradise might have been created.

Belief is a very strong power that we cannot underestimate. Belief is a doctrine that a person or a group accepts as true. People from different cultures have different beliefs and or superstitions. Some people grew up with the belief that certain consultations with a spiritual master must be done before any new business ventures. Some believe certain sacrifices must be made before any new business venture may be successful. Other people from other cultures imbibe their religious beliefs/superstitions into their day to day lives.

Imagine a situation where a prospective scam victim initially consults a spiritual master who informs him or her that the new business venture he or she is embarking on will materialize successfully, that it has been seen in the spiritual realm. This information from the spiritual realm is enough to make such believing prospective victim pursue the new business with all vigor for the rest of his or her life. What if such new business venture was a scam? There have been cases where many people became scam victims because their cultural superstitious beliefs have always inferred that they will be billionaires. They have grown up from day one with this believe and will not be so surprised if such an opportunity to realize this long belief presents itself as a genuine business looking scam.

When Mr. Zheng received the business proposal (scam business proposal), he quickly consulted his spiritual master in a Chinese temple, whom he has known for over 20 years. After due spiritual consultations and prayers, the spiritual master reliably informed Mr. Zheng that his new business venture will be successful. Mr. Zheng now went all out for the new business and in the process lost over $5,000,000 to the scammers.

You will understand here that it was the victim beliefs that cushioned the whole scam. The scammer did not have to do much work, because the driving motive was already present. The targeted commitment of Mr. Zheng was religious, as a matter of fact.

Many of us have different interpretations of good fortunes and misfortunes. It can be interpreted as spiritual gifts or spiritual bad luck.

Scam occultism introduced by the scammer can be an end game with complex psychology. When the scam victim has shown all the required commitments, followed all the scammer's directives, has made all requested finale payments to the scammer, and such victim is financially exhausted but still has a life hope and very keen to succeed in the business, then the scammer is stuck because business conclusion cannot still be possible in scam businesses. The scammer at this stage will attempt to bring in occultism by trying to ***use a belief as the excuse for non-materialization of the business***. The scammer, at this stage, is also stuck because damage has been done to the victim; it might not be possible to make more money out of the victim again, which is the main purpose of the whole and entire scam business. Having realized this, the scammer has to end the business. The scammer can do this by bringing in a finale payment request that the victim cannot handle or telling the victim that something spiritual is forcing the business not to materialize.

Let us also understand that the relationship between the scammer and the victim is like a hostage-terrorist relationship, both depending on the other's understanding. The addition here being that only one part (scammer) understands that the expected end gain is not possible and can never materialize. So, the scammer's only wish when it is clear that the victim is out financially (the purpose of the whole scheme defeated) is for the victim to go away, forget the whole business or pay more. Consider also, that there is no way the scammer will know if the victim is truly broke financially, since the scammer might not know the victim's total asset worth or even the victim's financial accessibility, so the scammer brings in occultism in the form of religion or beliefs to either make the victim forget the business and past payments or pay more to the scammer.

It is common for the authorities to underestimate the effect of these manipulations. It is at this stage of the scamming that the scam victims get into many ill-doings and crimes of which society becomes aware. Scam victims played into this occultism will either do the 'unexpected' to raise the money for the finale payment to finalize the business, or accept defeat and quit the business.

When scammers employ occultism, it has a way of bringing out the whole truth about the scam victim if that scam victim is a true

believer in the business (unknown scam). It is like casting a spell on the scam victim to succeed in the business or quit the business.

Faith and belief will make most people do what they will never do under normal circumstances. As Mr. Zheng's belief made him go into the scam business whole heartedly, so can the scammer tell the victim that their business is not working due to certain spiritual manipulations that must be cleared to see this business go through successfully. Such a believing victim will simply ask 'what should I do' and do it without questioning.

These same hypnotic occult manipulations are very common in certain religions where the religious leaders or congregation overseer's directives are strictly followed and obeyed without an atom of doubt. In very successful scams, the scammers achieved this level of occult manipulations on their scam victims, totally controlling them. So many crimes in societies are being promoted by this kind of occult manipulations. These occult directives can lead virtually to anything. Such directives are given mainly by the cult leader (scammer) for the scammer's own profit but executed by the manipulated cult member (victim).

Occultism may not involve rituals, sacrifices, incantation or the occult dance as most of us see it. So many scam victims are not just in scam businesses, but in scam occultisms they do not even know about. These occult manipulations might involve only simple day to day directives but the obedience, belief and faith in following these directives makes it occultism.

For twenty two years, Mr. Quinn and his wife always had done things together as husband and wife. They had always shared love and unity in their family. In two years and seven months, Mr. Quinn lost his and his wife's joint savings of $520,000 paying scammers without ever telling his wife what he was doing with their life savings money. They still lived in the same house, all the while Mr. Quinn carried on with the business. The wife always believed their money was safe for their retirement until two years and seven months later when the scam business was exposed to the wife.

Mr. Quinn did not perform any physical occult ritual, sacrifice, incantation or dance with the scammer but it was occultism. For Mr. Quinn to have followed the strict confidentiality directive from the scammer to this level was pure occultism. It is definite that somehow, sometime, in Mr. Quinn's mind or thinking, he absolutely believed that telling his wife would ruin the ensuing business. This is the truth of what happened, and the scammer achieved this by psychological manipulation which has a place in occultism.

For several years, Mr. Quinn and his wife saved together, what on earth could now be so confidential that his wife must not know? Whatever this new business gain was going to be was still for Mr. Quinn and his wife, considering their years together, so she should have been worthy to share in the secret, if Mr. Quinn was reasoning well and not being psychologically manipulated by the scammer.

When two or more people come together to achieve a 'suspicious' goal', a kind of cult is formed and a strong bond will develop amongst them. This bonding amongst them makes confidentiality requests occultism in nature. Certain requests in such partnerships become part of the process of achieving their final suspicious goal and they are strictly adhered to by all partners. This sequence has been around for a very long time.

There are several other ways the scammer can use and enter the victim's mind psychologically. Scammers tell their victims all sorts of lies which, after several repetitions, the victims will start believing those lies to be true as the scam processes progress. In several cases, the scam victims will start to tell their own lies, not necessarily directed by the scammer, but out of their own convictions in order to maintain the agreed confidentiality as if an occult oath was taken in the new business venture. It is therefore very important that when a loved one is becoming very secretive about an imaginary business venture that more effort is exerted to uncover what is actually going on.

My roommate in the university kept waking up very early for several weeks. He would wake up by 6:00 am, go to town and come back to the campus by 8:00 am for our first lecture of the day. This continued for several weeks and whenever I asked, he always replied he had to see someone in town and never gave more details. After this usual response, he would smile at me and we'd go about our routine for the day. After some weeks, he then started asking me which kind of car I liked. We were young and Mercedes Benz was

one of the favorites then. So, I told him I liked Mercedes Benz to which he would agree, while I expected him to contradict me and for our normal arguments to ensue. There were no such arguments anymore, only his great smiles. I started noticing that he was gradually removing his belongings, his refrigerator, his textbooks, he was always financially broke and we had to manage with my little allowances. I kept wondering because it was not that bad with our backgrounds. Even after showing me some of the good cash he raised, the whole money would just vanish after these mysterious early town trips.

Finally one morning he woke me up and said that I should escort him to town. We stopped at a shop and bought two huge bags. He did not talk much on our way and simply went to a restaurant in town where we waited, from 7:00 am until 11:00 pm in the evening for someone who never came. I watched my friend's composure change totally as we waited. Around 11:00 pm he checked with a restaurant worker, and we were directed to go somewhere else to check on someone. We left by that time and got to one empty street. There we headed to a medium warehouse store, the gates of which were closed. We meticulously noted the store number and went back to campus. All this time he was still not saying much to me. The next morning we left early again and went straight to the store we noted the previous night. The problem now was that the empty street of yesterday night was now very busy with flourishing businesses. Even when we located the store, the store owner, a responsible-looking elderly man kindly asked us what we wanted. My friend inquired about one Silas and Clement. Politely the elderly man told us there were no such persons working for him and moreover he sold only electronics and not chemicals which were quite evident from the stocks in the store. My friend started shouting and claiming that it was in that very store he met Silas and Clement. It was a real problem until police finally came and we were taken away. The police later, let us go with serious warnings regarding mistaken identity. When we got back to campus we still did not discuss anything. It was as if a demonic spell had taken over my roommate.

Whatever happened really affected my friend because he was traumatized and lost an extra year in campus. I finished that very year and left for my national youth service. It was only two years ago while putting this book together that he accepted to narrate the whole story to me. Can you believe it; that was exactly 20 years after we left the university? From his detailed story, it was a clear case of 'wash money scam'. Some people he ran into wanted to clean black money for him. As a student then he lost a fortune; he sold a major part of his father's belongings and family assets without anyone's knowledge as he tried by all means possible to realize the business. Any money he could lay his hands on or came his way went straight to Silas and Clement. For a good child then, who was his parent's pride, my friend really hurt them so much, putting them into serious financial predicaments. The question was 'what was he doing with all the money' he realized by selling his parents properties. It took a year for his parents to figure out the whole lose and forgive him to go back to university and finish his education.

This is a good example of a scan business that had occultism. What on earth did these scammers (Silas and Clement) tell my friend that he could not tell me then, until 20 years later and the knowledge that I was doing this book? Upon, we were seeing each other regularly in those 20 years?

If you follow the story from the beginning, you will understand a particular pattern. The unclear attitude of the victim for several weeks, dedicated early morning wake ups, trips to town, the smiles and imaginations of success that would have benefited me too, if it had worked. It is important to note here that the entire victim's actions were positively intended to benefit me. He was not hiding the business from me for any bad reason whatsoever, his intentions should the business materialize were very honorable as a good friend. He was hiding the business from me so that the business would materialize successfully. Maybe telling me would ruin it—superstitious beliefs. This confidentiality directive must have been given to him by the scammers, but better modified by my friend as is common in most scams. A scam victim presently paying scammers has an unclear attitude towards his loved ones. A change in character, that confident smile of a new found solution. It is natural that what makes it difficult for loved ones to understand these changes in the victim's character is because the overall intentions presented by the victim is never to harm the loved ones but to surprise them with these new business gains. Like my friend who genuinely wanted to buy a Mercedes Benz for me if his business had been successful.

There have been cases where the scammer employed occultism to make the victim forget the business but the outcome was outrageous. A person fully committed to a genuine business can commit murder to see such businesses go through talk less of a fully committed scam victim, particularly when the victim is financially broke. There are cases where the scam victims are told by the scammer that the non-materialization of the business is spiritual. Some scam victims believe in fetishism and will believe anything the scammer says as long as it is a solution for the business to succeed. Underestimating a committed scam victim's will is always a problem most people and the authorities face. Without the basic knowledge that the business is a scam, a deeply committed scam victim can do anything for the business success. This disposition is even more severe after losing so much money to the unknown scammers.

In physically introduced scams, it is easier for the scammer to read the victim's psychological make-up and introduce the occultism, making such scam very dangerous. Examples of dangerous scams in society are **secret cults**, **secret** fraternities, **secret** sororities, etc. A closer observation will show that the leaders of these cults are always the richest. Other cult members are like scam victims, since their cult leaders scam them with levies, dues, fees, contributions, directives, messages, etc., and even threaten these scam victims with violence for non compliance.

The confidentiality directive in scam when obeyed is like an oath taken in an occult sect. This oath might not have been taken physically but the understanding between the scammer and the victim was the same as an occult oath.

Victims in scam businesses look possessed by a kind of demon; the scam victim feels suddenly very wise and full of expectations. It is always like the solution that will make the victim's life better has just arrived, but he or she is not disclosing it to the observer. The memory of my friend's countenance is still very vivid in my mind. He was always full of smiles and always saw expensive things as nothing in our minor arguments as students then. He seemed then to have future solution to all financial problems, including mine.

The acceptance to keep confidentiality in a business is the oath taking if that business is a scam and it is common in most successful scams. This is quite different from business secrets, technology secrets and industrial secrets. The confidentiality kept in scam businesses are quite different in the sense that you are expected to keep this secret from even your loved ones, who would also benefit from the promised gain and could have advised you, better.

Another observation is that the scam victim can hardly explain how he or she started keeping these secrets. The scammer's design makes keeping these secrets automatic; by the time the scam victim keeps four to five secrets, the rest becomes automatic and the victim is soon keeping twenty secrets. I discovered that the scammers did not remind their victims to keep the sixth and seventh secrets; these victims knew automatically, and where possible manufactured suitable cover lies on their own.

Also, it is while the victim is maintaining confidentiality, that the scammer will design every stage of the business (unknown scam business) process to have a near conclusion in sight, which makes the victim further postpone the idea of informing anyone. *'Why inform them now, after all by early next week the promised gains will be in my pocket'.* This notion can run for a very long time, such as it did for Mr. Quinn; two years and seven months. It is normal that by the time the victim opens up to anyone, enough damage has been done.

Maintaining confidentiality in an unknown business is like a cult oath taking, which becomes occult if that unknown business is a scam.

CHAPTER 24

THE EFFECTIVENESS OF THE SCAM NETWORKS

The majority of scams worrying the world are networked. Scam businesses are now being set up like genuine businesses with branches spread over major cities. Do not be surprised that a scam operating elsewhere has a branch office in your neighborhood, and do not always expect a physical office but be sure that people of similar intentions are in your neighborhood. Deceit can be nursed in the mind and remain unexposed.

Scam is a business based on individualities of the scam victims on one part and their scammers on the other. Initially, the believe was that scams operate from a particular place or country, but it is now clear that scam businesses are now operating practically all over the planet, working with a marvelous network the authorities seem not to understand clearly.

In some successful big scam stories, I have observed that the networking also added credibility to the scamming process. These observations showed that the scammer's usage of another territory, or different locations, cleared some of the scam victim's doubts. Most scam victims believed the scammer's story better if developed countries like Japan, Switzerland, USA, France and the UK were mentioned in the transaction as contact points or branches, instead of the scammer concentrating the whole scam operation in only one country. Likewise, the mention and involvement of different nationals in the ensuing business (scam) has been observed to give scam victims further confidence in the business. You will discover that most big scams involved different persons, different location and different nationals. These are rampant in investment scams, lottery scams, 'wash money' scams and money transfer scams, to mention only a few.

A scam victim in a scan business can be directed to anywhere in the world and the scam business will still continue. This possibility has only added credibility in the way scam victims see these unknown scam schemes. Scam network which is a network of scammers with the same intention have this ability. Anything that will satisfy the scam victim to pay the scammer can be manufactured no matter where. Observations show that many victims were better convinced when they were told to visit a finance company in central London to collect their money than when they were told to visit another finance company in Kampala. Most well articulated large scams in progress are networked and this networking has a way of disarming victims as many think certain things are not possible in certain vicinities. Networking makes it possible for the same scammer to connect with other scammers in other cities including the victim's indigenous country or place of residence. It is easy for a seasoned scammer to get a partner even in the victim's locality.

A good number of your present neighbors where you live will see it as no big deal to deliver a trunk box to your house address and collect a previously settled $50,000 from you, to keep $25,000 and send the balance ($25,000) to their scammer partner they might not have met before. Crime businesses can have this level of trust.

Scammers are also in your neighborhood for your information and they will be very fast in ripping you off, too. A good number of people in your locality will do the above errand for the $25,000, which is a lot of money.

What makes this errand easy to accomplish is that the scammer had ***previously arranged the exchange*** with the victim perfectly, either on the phone, via email or with documentations. There will be not much talk or questioning from the victim. Just 'deliver the box and collect the money, keep 50% and send 50%'. The scammer and the scammer's partner might never have seen each other but the 50-50 sharing ratio is enough to build a stronger trust between them, than is seen in regular genuine business partnerships.

In another perspective, ***the cost of scamming*** $50,000 from a victim is negligible to the scammer unlike in genuine businesses. A genuine business of $50,000 turnover will involve a measurable cost. Even a 1000% profit, will mean $5,000 costs. But in scam business, to get a $50,000 turnover might involve only a $50 telephone call. So, the scammer can easily forgo half of the turnover to a scammer-partner and still make unbelievable profit. This is another factor that makes scam networks very effective unlike genuine business where the costs are fully considered and cannot be forgone easily.

In most scams that have been extended to the victims' localities, the scammers' partners in those victims' localities preferred their own premises to avoid complications. A scammer can also get the scam victim's fellow countrymen to assist in the scamming. Some victims find it difficult to believe that their fellow countrymen will join in such scam scheme. The promise of good financial reward can drive anything is something most people must understand.

Many scam victims have confessed to deliberately involving their relations in scam businesses to be scammed. They did this to recover their past losses in other scams after they discovered theirs was a scam or after the scammer purposely exposed the scam scheme to the victim out of pity for being financially broke. Such victims were encouraged to bring in fellow associates and countrymen for a certain percentage share of the extorted gains. Such scam cases are special and always very successful because they are scams based on strong trust.

In analyzing scam networks, we must understand that there are people of same ethnic groups living in different countries all over the world. People of different ethnicities are now in the same country plying their livelihoods. Contacts can be made and harnessed. For instances, Chinese products and services in Shanghai can also be obtained in China towns in the USA. A traditional South African dance can also be performed in London by South Africans living in London. A scammer can have friends of similar intentions in Moscow and those friends in Moscow can have indigenous Muscovites of similar intentions as friends, too.

Moreover, if you have observed as I have, there seems to be a special bond that binds evil doers all over the world. One should wonder how a thief locates another thief even in a totally new environment. No matter how secluded one thief is and the environment he or she is in, you will be surprised how that thief will locate another thief living in the same neighborhood. It is a mystery to me but just the truth. This automatic bonding needs no formal introduction or explanation, it just gums when evil doers meet and it is the mystery of evil doing. People who reason alike have a special way of knowing each other. The reason for this, I do not know, but they just identify each other the moment they meet, even on the phone, and together they resume their trades as partners.

The saying that 'among thieves there is honor' is a strong binding force in scammers' networks. Without meeting themselves physically, scam networks work perfectly with an astonishing success rate based on trust. The ease in getting the victim's money and sharing of the victim's finale payments between scammers are binding factors in most scam business networks. It makes it possible for Ms. Ade, who is a scammer in Lagos to comfortably release her prospective victim's information to Mr. Bruce who is another scammer in London. They have not met before but there is trust that Mr. Bruce in London will deliver and Ms. Ade in Lagos will definitely get her share of the scam victim's payment once the scam is successful.

Another reality is that a scam victim seems to believe anything that will lead to a favorable conclusion of the business. It is therefore common that since conclusion in a scam business is not possible; that the scammer might at particular stages in the business process, change the storyline for the victim to continue believing the scammer's stories. Scammers can do this by changing the locality of the next transaction in the business (scam). I think scammers also use deadlines shift to rearrange their scams, possibly relocating the venue of the scam.

Mr. Johnson, an American businessman, was told that his long awaited lottery winning was now to be processed in the firm's office in New York. He was relieved that this might eventually materialize at least now that it was closer to home. He continued following the scammer's instructions and the New York lottery official's instructions until he lost another $48,000. Mr. Johnson could not believe that the New York lottery official he was talking to in New York was also a scammer; the accent, spoken English, manners, etc., were all perfect and beyond suspicion.

The majority of people are more comfortable at home and this makes many people get scammed easily. Home feeling sooths such victims and in most cases the loss in guard is very significant.

So many police authorities have always visualized scams as mafia like organized crimes but I think they are not. I think scammers operate individually or in small cells of two to three people. They only network other scammers or cells where necessary. It is also this uniqueness of scam businesses that makes it difficult to catch their perpetrators.

Scammers can abandon all their work equipments and vanish. Scammers can operate from anywhere; train, station, airplane, bus, office, walkway, toilet, etc. Their networks cannot be easily infiltrated by the police because it does not really exist as envisaged by the police. Somebody planning to deceive you in a business relationship can have it in mind, smile with you and wait patiently for the business to commence. It is unlike the mafia organizations where enforcers carry guns and stern looking faces. The mafia enforcer needs guns and force, while the deceiver needs no compulsory equipments, and at worst, the deceiver's equipments are also used in genuine businesses. Deceit is relative to its premise; it is not like managing distribution of illicit drugs or management of enforcers, as seen in drug cartels and mafia respectively.

Deceit has survived over time because it has never been fully organized or headed by anyone somewhere.

If scams are mafia like, I do not think, I will be receiving the same scam proposal email from five different persons within a month. Scammers are simply on random sampling for scam targets who will become prospective scam victim. Moreover, the scammer is not forcing you to comply with the business proposal like the mafias do. No matter the pre-information about a scam target, and the perfect way the scam proposal was presented, the scam target can still refuse to do the business and the scammer cannot force the scam target unlike the mafias.

The individualities of both the scammer and the scam victim must be considered in every successful scam, because each successful scam is unique. This is why a scam victim might not pay one scammer a cent but pay another scammer millions for the same similar scam proposal. I think the real picture is that every scammer based on his or her own scamming method and skills, is randomly searching for his or her ideal scam victim in a world where scam targets are infinite and their financial abilities infinite, too. Scammers do not fight for territories nor do they fight for scam victims because both are infinite. I do not think scammers have an overall boss scammer to account to, such as in a mafia organization.

Mr. Alibe, a very successful scammer, might be living in a well furnished duplex in New York, making his millions of dollars in scams. Another scammer, Mr. Wade, a not yet very successful scammer, is living in a one room apartment in Ouagadougou making hundreds of dollars in scams. Mr. Alibe might be scamming Ms. Philips on an investment scam while Mr. Wade might be scamming the same Ms. Philips on a lottery scam. They do not know each other and territory pose no conflicts for them, because Ms. Philips can do both businesses simultaneously. Mr. Alibe and Mr. Wade can even be scamming Ms. Philips on the same investment scam originating from different proposals and localities. Both scammers do not know each other and might never meet. It is only when a prospective scam victim of Mr. Wade is New York based (or needs a New York scam stage) which Mr. Alibe's services will provide adequately. It is only then that they go in search and might exchange information for a successful scamming of the New York based prospective victim and share their gains as agreed. If Mr. Alibe gets arrested in New York by the police, he does not know Mr. Wade in details and the police authorities might not believe him.

I observed this in Mrs. Taylor's story.

It was after a long investigation that the Melbourne police realized that Mr. Jackson, a convicted scammer only extorted $22,000 from Mrs. Taylor. Mrs. Taylor had previously lost $312,000 in that very scam business to other scammers. Mr. Jackson only had their telephone numbers.

I think what happened here was that, the earlier unknown scammers presently at large must have forwarded Mrs. Taylor's (victim) information to Mr. Jackson in Melbourne to continue the scamming since Mrs. Taylor was based there before the police moved in on Mr. Jackson.

The organization in scam businesses should be seen as scam networks, and not mafia organizations. Scam networking has also brought in mafia style violence within the scam networks; there have been news or rumors that some scammers killed other scammers for not releasing their shares of the scam victim's payment. Such violence is common in very high profit businesses like scams. I have also come across stories where scam victims will purposely claim they made exaggerated payments when it is not true, causing problems for the scammers, resulting in fights the authorities know. A scammer can easily setup a fellow scammer with a supposed prospective victim who is the police. So many such cases have been reported to the authorities, when scammers get greedy on their scam partners, contrary to the network trust.

Most reported scam stories show one common thing when these fights emerge among scammers; no matter the confidentiality treaty in any scam business, no matter the oath of silence the scam victim has taken or the scam occultism used, all these will break as soon as the victim realizes beyond reasonable doubt that the whole business is a scam and that the promised gain is not coming in any form. The only way to keep any scamming secret is for the scammer to ensure that the promised gain eventually gets to the scam victim.

This has been the case for corrupt leaders of some countries, when they made several genuine money transfers in the past. *A successful money transfer business can remain a secret forever because it was successful and all parties involved are happy.* In reality, so many past and present government officials of some countries have siphoned stolen funds out of their countries using money transfers schemes, most of the information and transactions in the past never came to light because in actuality, those funds were really transferred and the foreign facilitators were well compensated. Of course it was real human beings not computers that assisted those leaders and government officials steal their countries blind. Had it been those money transfer transactions then did not materialize for real; maybe we all would have long known that some money transfer schemes were scams. As a matter of fact, there are still genuine money transfer schemes going on presently, and the news is fuelling similar money transfer scams.

Scams generally are facilitated by both advantageous networks and disadvantageous networks worldwide. It is such networks that make it possible for a bank guarantee issued to a scammer via an American scam victim's bank can be discounted in a mega bank in Europe. Such networks make it possible for a scam victim's $2,500,000 payment in Australia, to be made available to the scammers in Spain, without raising an eyebrow in anti money laundry circles. The same kind of networking, in some cases, makes it impossible for you to recover the funds you lost to scammers.

Mr. Eriksson, a scam victim, insisted to the police authorities that he paid the money into a government account; he was right because the beneficiary of the said account was a government establishment. After several investigations, it was discovered that the government official impersonator, who opened the account in the Caribbean bank, withdrew all deposits cash and closed the account officially one hour after Mr. Eriksson money wire was credited to the account. Mr. Eriksson was reporting the theft three months later. Upon the photograph of the impersonator was available, it was still complicated locating him. The authorities have declared the impersonator wanted and they are still searching.

Of course the authorities are doing their best but it is difficult to make people vomit what they have already digested. The scam network is complex, because, there are so many genuine persons in genuine positions, who assist or facilitate such scammed funds for a share and they are all over the world. The major beneficiary of a huge scam was once named the best customer of the mega bank through which the scam funds passed. How can the authorities get banks to start refunding bank charges on confirmed scam funds? How do the authorities get money transfer firms to refund commissions on which they have already balanced their annual accounts?

Anyone wishing to avoid scams cannot underestimate the capabilities of scam networks. Scams could have not been possible without these networks. Scams usually involve money and most people like making money. Moreover, everyone has been seriously warned against falling for scams. These warnings are everywhere that you cannot say you have not come across one at least. The only short fall is that these warnings cannot and will never cover all the different forms of scams the world is seeing now, nor cover the processes involved in these scams.

The reality is that when you get scammed, you have made yourself 'a kill' for an animal kingdom of various carnivorous animals. Many genuine institutions will be involved in getting the scam victim's money to the scammer. Some workers in these genuine institutions will act deliberately and some unknowingly in ensuring the scammer gets the scam victim's money. There will be banks chasing commissions, bureau de change chasing exchange profits, corrupt authorities who get settled, facilitators chasing agreed commissions, corrupt finance firms, corrupt online banks collecting commissions, etc. Many will be involved directly and indirectly for their respective monetary gains.

Many genuine institutions through which scam monies passed cannot and will not vomit what they have digested. Many of such genuine financial institutions only bother about their commissions and costs of transfer, losing such gained business profits, due to the scam nature of the ensuing transaction, might seem unnecessary to them. The majority of these institutions have shareholders who want dividends. After all, everyone has been seriously warned to avoid scams.

Summarily, scam networks have aided scams and most major scams are well networked. Many persons and entities are involved in networked scams knowingly and unknowingly.

CHAPTER 25

THE IMAGINATION AND REALIZATION STRUGGLE

The scam victim does not fail to imagine what he or she will do with the promised gains of the business (scam) which inhibits his or her realization of the actual present situation he or she is in. The imagination and realization struggle is unmistakable for most victims of scam businesses. This struggle might be unnoticeable because the same feature appears in some genuine businesses, minus the secrecy which is peculiar to scam businesses.

Unlike in genuine businesses, these imaginations in scam businesses are tailored by the scammer's offer subconsciously. Normally, it is underestimated, so I have decided to treat it here. I regard it as important in understanding what happens to almost all victims of scam businesses. The scam victim cannot realize what an outsider can realize about the business in which the victim is involved.

Nine out of every ten scam victims had imaginations that made it impossible for them to realize the scam situations in which they were involved. The imagination of the scam victim during the scamming is one of the major forces behind getting that victim scammed. It is actually what any loved one should look out for when you are suspecting a loved one of being scammed or in a scam business. Such victims never fail to promise a surprise package for relations and friends.

These imaginations or visions; what the victim will do with the incoming money, what he or she will buy, the new image he or she will have, etc., will occupy the victim's thoughts as long as the scam business progresses. Such victims will hide these imaginations or visions as much as possible but many of the signs will still show, like making exaggerated promises to loved ones. They are visions based on the promised gain coming in the business he or she does not know is a scam. These same imaginations or visions will also develop in the victim's subconscious, irrespective of how rich that scam victim already is. This is the irony of human greed. Even a multi-millionaire will still have these imaginations for a mere $1 million, he or she is expecting from a suspicious business (scam)

I strongly believe these imaginations and visions originate from the surrounding irregularities of a scam business. Scam proposals portray uncommon businesses; something uncommon can also be something improper, which can be something illegal. The irregularities in a scam business proposal might not be pronounced initially but prospective victims in a scam business process know it exists. They know the business is uncommon, they know the business is irregular and they know the business is improper, and which are enough to make them likewise nurse the idea that the business might be illegal.

Let us look at this situation;

Mr. Berth's imagination of the benevolence he will do for the nearby charity was such that he even wrote a post dated cheque to the charity. This great benevolence made him pursue the business with all vigor and in the process of trying to realize this promise he lost close to $300,000 to the scammers and the business still did not materialize.

This is a good example of what the imagination involved in scam businesses can lead you to. It can make you promise things you would never have promised, if the business was genuine. In genuine businesses, majority will make such promises after conclusion of the business but in scam businesses the urge to be benevolent is always very pronounced. In most cases, these benevolences from scam victims have a psychological backing that arises from these scam victims' perception of guilt and illegality in the gains of the ensuing business (scam).

A guilty conscience is always afraid and tries to pacify. Expecting a gain you know you have not earned can create a guilty conscience. Expecting a huge income for a little input as most scam businesses portray has a psychological effect on those scam victims. Scam victims clearly know that their input into the business is meager when compared to what they are expecting to gain, creating guilt somehow. Mr. Berth above may have given the post dated cheque to the charity, so that God would know his clean mind and see to it that the business ends successfully.

It is common for people making irregular business profits to perform outrageous acts of charity. Irregular businesses in this sense are businesses with very high profits and uncommon rates of return, which are out of authorized regulations. For instance, if the cost of production is $10 each and the producer is selling the product for $1000 each, then expect outrageous acts of charities from the producer.

Scam proposals have undertones of irregularities that receivers cannot deny.

There is always something 'not common' in scam proposals. 'Not common' can also be irregular or 'illegal'. Read any scam proposal again or review a past successful scam and you cannot tell me that something uncommon, which can be termed irregular or even illegal, is not contained in the proposal or in the past scam process.

This is also applicable to HYIP scams. The fact to keep in mind here is that, you and I both know to invest $100 and get $160 after two days is not very common, and is not very applicable in the majority of genuine businesses. So, when you have invested such an amount in a scam HYIP, the same imagination or vision we discussed earlier will still enter your subconscious because you know what you are doing is very uncommon, irregular and might be illegal. Your subconscious will always ask the question, 'what is this HYIP using my $100 investment for in two days that is generating this huge profit?' which you will never answer yourself as an investor expecting an unworthy gain. You might think you have deceived your mind, who thinks the HYIP is investing your money is something uncommon, improper or irregular. Remember that the undertone of a scam proposal implies that the business emanates from the premises of irregular businesses, uncommon businesses or illegality infested genuine businesses.

Our subconscious has a way of perceiving what is regular and irregular; it is not easy to deceive our minds by pretending we do not know it is irregular on the outside when our inside knows it is irregular and can be illegal.

It only creates a scammer's paradise when we try to deceive our minds. When a victim's mind feels it is somehow irregular, the victim's boldness will diminish, making it easier for the scammer to completely control the victim. This is always the case no matter how often the victim claims outwardly that the business is regular or legal.

Do not pretend you do not know what the illicit drug dealer does with the money you lend him. You clearly understand that $100 investment cannot genuinely generate $160 in two days, but you invested in the suspicious business nonetheless. You are simply creating an inability to properly declare the truth due to the perceived irregularity. If your mind says it is blue, then it is blue, whether you pronounce red or green from your mouth does not matter, but your actions will still show what your mind believes—it's blue.

Any business that is unusual with high margins of profit to be made can easily trigger an unexpected imagination in a participant, which will make proper realization of the present situation difficult. This is exactly what happens in scam businesses. The scam victim's imaginations are what hamper the realization that the whole business is a scam. When what a prospective victim or victim will do with the expected gain has fully occupied that victim's thoughts, then it will become difficult for that victim to realize any suspicious process in the business, which might indicate the business is a scam.

Most scam victims will hurt you if you carelessly inform them that their beloved business venture is a scam. Such scam victims can only be told such bad news skillfully or you might cause more harm to that victim or even cause that victim to harm the informing party.

Realization is what will enable the victim to deduce if the business is scam or what to do about it, but when the victim's imaginations have entirely blocked avenues for this realization, then a serious problem has been created.

Imaginations or visions and their abilities to hinder realization are very common in most successful scams and would be successful scams.

CHAPTER 26

THE ADAMANT PROGRESSIVES

'Winners never quit'.
'Success is allied to the brave'.

These might be facts but not applicable in all cases, particularly in unknown transactions.

When one has been in a business transaction very long, you will notice that the person's desire becomes getting progress in the business transaction and not necessarily materialization of the business. This is applicable in scam situations too, after a long period of scamming, the scam victim simply wants to hear that the business *has progressed to another level and not necessarily that it has materialized*. If the scam business has processes, then the movement from one process to the other will simply become the business. Such scam victims are adamant progressive and they rarely ask when the business will materialize. Adamant progressives believe business processes go step by step which is true, but in scams, the scammer can elongate and keep elongating the business processes.

Unknown situations are difficult to assess without a proven assessment method. The first step to knowledge is the willingness to learn, keeping your previous knowledge aside. Committing ourselves to any endeavor requires that what we are striving for is worth the commitment. You just cannot keep on trying if the venture is a scam. It is therefore important to be sure that whatever business venture you are pursuing is not a scam before persistence becomes your new rule.

We have discussed so many features of scams that can be used to detect scam business, but some people presently in scam businesses, who come across this book will not apply the test with these scam features described on their present businesses, instead, they will only try to point out where these scam business features differ from their own present businesses, which they do not know are scams. What they really want is for the business they are in to keep progressing from one stage to another and not necessarily conclude. The knowledge that the business is progressing somehow gives them hope. They are the adamant progressives. The majority of scam victims make up this group.

In most scams I have analyzed, the scam victims thought a symbiotic relationship existed between them and the scammers, while the scammers knew they were parasitic relationships. The commitment levels of scam victims are based on a symbiotic relationship where both parties will eventually gain from the association. Ultimately, the only gainer is the scammer. I would rather say that this relationship between scammers and their victims is a mixture of dual desires as seen in some negotiations. Both parties are trying to maximize their gains. One thing unique in scams is that the gain of the scammer is unlimited and can always be altered to increase or decrease as the scammer wishes, while the gain of the victim is fixed and can only decrease as the victim expends in the scam business or the business lasts longer. I also observed that for the victim's promised gain in a scam business to increase, it must be re-introduced afresh by the scammer via another proposal like the initial proposal the scammer sent to the prospective victim.

The adamant progressives are very common in successful scams, since they see the business as something to persist in that will eventually materialize, as it progresses from process to process, not knowing it is a scam. They therefore, put in all their best efforts and do all that is expected of them hoping it will work out. They end up being in the same business with the same expectations for many years. Many scam victims stay in the business for 3 years, some 5 years and possibly a lifetime. They just will never let go. The business must materialize as each process is overcome, making them think they have earned the success of the business.

Unknown scam can last long and when such scam business has stayed for so long without materializing, you will start to wonder why a reasonable person should still be in the same business. My inferences show that most scam victims have been in a scam business for so many years because of the *Insider Information Effect.*

As a new contractor, I often wondered why some contractors should allow their due payments for completed contracts to be owed by the government for so many years. Many contractors just kept quiet and waited patiently for the payment for several years. It was later on that I discovered that each of such owed contractors had someone (an insider) they trusted to inform them accurately on the awaited payment. This was the reason why they waited patiently. This person they trusted was either working with them in their own contracting organization or was working with the governmental organization that owed them. Put simply, they all had someone they trusted to keep them properly informed on inside information on their awaited contract payment.

I have clearly observed that in every successful scam that has lasted for so long, there was someone beyond suspicion the scam victim trusted either in the scam victim's own organization or in the scammer's organization. The unusual duration of the business (scam) was possible due to this trusted person's information to the scam victim.

Normal occurrence is that after sometime, a scam victim might start to suspect the business, but the insider will always cushion this suspicion with insider information. The insider does this by giving the victim very privileged information on the ensuing business transaction (scam). This privileged information acts like a sale of confidence such as the one initially sold to the victim by the scammer's first proposal. This renewal of sale of confidence is based on the absolute trust. Whether the privileged information is right or wrong is part of another discussion entirely.

As a contractor, I normally call on my friend who worked in the accounting department of the very ministry that owed my company; he informed me reliably that the governmental ministry will pay our contractors' batch by cheque payment. I believed him without any doubt and traveled outside the country on another business. It was after several months when I came back, that I discovered my other colleagues were all paid the very next month following my departure via ePayments directly into their company accounts.

I now had to apply for ePayment, wait for another payment batch which took another year even though I had a good trusted friend who worked there directly. I used to give my friend gifts to inform me accurately. It was not a bribe but a motivator to keep watch, possibly collect my cheque and pay it into my account. I called several times from abroad and he had my telephone number. For five months, he did not deem it fit to inform me that other contractors of my batch have been paid. I even bought presents for him on my way back. My questions are these, is it possible he did not know, and was he scamming me? Is he guilty of anything?

Everyone will have to find out first, if that long business in which one is involved is a scam. If it is, then you must endeavor to locate the insider causing the insider information effect. The insider might be your trusted assistant or advisor. Rule no one out. It might also be a person you came across on the scammer's side. In most cases, the insider causing the insider information effect on the scam victim is someone who has previously created that impeccable impression on the victim. He or she is deemed to be above suspicions and the victim trusts him or her fully.

Some encouragers can cause the same insider information effect unknowingly.

A loved one might have encouraged you to go into that business which eventually you discovered to be a scam.

This is also an insider information effect but done unknowingly as an encourager.

Most adamant progressives last that long in the scam businesses due to the insider information effect. It is important for every person, who has been in a particular business, for very long, to locate this insider causing the insider information effect, so that the person could visualize the business transaction better.

Maybe I should have directly asked the Accountant General in that ministry when our contractor batch would be paid instead of trusting my good friend who worked there too. But the very first day I visited the ministry to process my payment after the contract completion, my same friend took me personally inside the computer room and showed me my company name scheduled for payment.

Currently there are many adamant progressives in several scams worldwide. They have been in that very business for so long and will never believe it is a scam. They will still do the business tomorrow and the next until it materializes. They are winners all their lives so they never quit. Yes, no matter what, they will finally win—if there is something to win!. Unfortunately, there is nothing a scam victim can win in a scam because it is a scam. No matter how real it appears, and no matter the personalities involved, a scam remains a scam and there is nothing to gain in it for the scam victim.

You will have to know first if your unknown transaction is a scam. If it is a scam then quit. If it has been long, try to locate the insider carefully. He or she is definitely somewhere near you, then quit and forget the whole business or pursue recovery legally if you can. Do not spend a penny more on anything concerning that same business. Likewise, forget the insider, no matter who it is. If the insider is a loved one, narrate the whole story and if he or she insists you should continue the business, assume this loved one to be a scammer you never thought was one and you are safe.

PART 4

SCAM BUSINESS AS A CRIME.

Scams are morally wrong and they are crimes punishable by law. This is the norm all over the world, yet in few cases are the culprits punished by law. In this part we now look at the legalities and illegalities involved in the crime of deceit and why some governments have taken them seriously and while some other governments have taken them lightly.

Bear in mind that the majority of scams do not involve defined goods for which explicit receipts of payment can be issued. The court has laws to look at, and the judge being human, will try to deduce to a great extent what must have transpired between the victim and the scammer. The scam victim's main problem in a court of law is one of conviction; the victim and scammer must not be seen as partners in a 'suspicious' business, (irregular, uncommon, improper, or illegal business).

CHAPTER 27

LAWS ON SCAMS AND FRAUDS

Scammers achieve their intentions of extorting their victims by imitating genuine business transaction processes. As long as we all understand that scam business transactions imitate genuine business transactions, then, there are basic laws that prohibit certain business practices and processes even in genuine business transactions, which are locally and internationally accepted. Although, many victims are not aware of these basic laws which can help scam victims in successfully prosecuting their scammers.

It is common that most scammers will plan their scams in very different ways to deceive their unsuspecting victims into paying them money or releasing their private details, but primarily almost all scams display something illegal that has a law against it in most nations worldwide.

In as much as a scam victim might not be able, to explain in full details the whole business transactions to the authorities, but a careful analysis of the ensued business will indicate that one of the below mentioned laws was breached. This is common in almost all confirmed scam business transactions. It is generally accepted that there are categorically, laws that prohibit;

Misleading or deceptive conduct; It is unlawful for a business or person to engage in conduct which is misleading or deceptive, or which is likely to mislead or deceive. This covers conduct that is likely to create a misleading overall impression among the audience about, for example, the price, value or quality of goods or services.

Representations about business activities; It is unlawful for a business or person to make false or misleading representations about the availability, nature or the terms and conditions of employment or the profitability, risk or other material aspect of any business activity that requires work or investment by others. Examples—work from home and business opportunity scams may be misleading by guaranteeing an impossible income, or by misleading you about what is involved in the 'job'.

Failure to provide relevant information; It is unlawful for a business or person to withhold relevant information that will aid better judgment of the participants in a business transaction. Failing to disclose relevant information, promises, opinions and predictions can also be misleading or deceptive. Most scams violate this law in general.

Wrongly accepting payments for goods or services; It is unlawful for a business or person to accept payment for goods or services they do not intend to supply. Examples—classifieds and online scams where scammers offer cut price goods that they have no intention to supply.

Offering rebates, gifts, prizes and other free items; It is unlawful when promoting goods or services to offer gifts, prizes or other free items if the business or person does not intend to, or does not, provide them as offered. Examples—Lottery scams, competition scams where the scammer falsely tells the prospective victim that they have won a prize to elicit an upfront payment or their personal information.

Misleading representations with respect to future matters; It is unlawful for a business or person to make a representation about a future matter with no reasonable grounds for making the representation. Examples—prize or merchandise offers, online auction scams, 'free' offers on the internet, betting scams and some office supply scams. For instance, a betting scam that offers you guaranteed winnings may be misleading as it is not possible to accurately predict the outcome of an event that is based on chance.

False or misleading representations; It is unlawful for a business or person to make false or misleading representations about goods or services when supplying, offering to supply or promoting goods or services. It is also unlawful to make or use false or misleading testimonials. This includes claims about the age, quality, sponsorship, approval, price or benefits of the goods or services. Examples—miracle cures scams.

Unsolicited supply of goods or services; It is unlawful for a business or person to request payment for goods or services that you have not ordered or for unauthorized entries or advertisements. Example, false billing scams.

Unconscionable conduct; It is unlawful to act unconscionably in a business transaction. These include serious misconduct or something clearly unfair or unreasonable conducts which ignores conscience or conduct that is not right or reasonable. Conduct can also be unconscionable in relation to the bargaining power of the parties involved in a transaction, or if someone is clearly under a "special disadvantage" (which has included a disability, a lack of English skills, a chronic illness or poor literacy and numeracy skills). Example, some miracle cure scams. Other conduct that scammers may participate in—such as exerting unfair pressure on you to buy their product or selling products that are exorbitantly priced—might also breach this law.

If you have the right knowledge, a clear understanding of the right steps to take in any unknown transaction, and you are meticulously monitoring the unknown business processes, you will not be easily scammed. Scamming you will have to involve some legalities, which will make your case genuine in any court of competent jurisdiction.

CHAPTER 28

LEGALITIES AND ILLEGALITIES

Scams have been defined as schemes for making money by dishonest means; it is also to obtain money or other goods from somebody by dishonest means. Scams are illegal and can never be legitimate but there are serious complications in scams that often complicate the prosecution of the perpetrators of these crimes.

One fact that is basic and complicates scams is that; in most cases, the victims gave the money to the scammer willingly. Scam victims often cannot prove that they were under duress to give the scammer money. The scammer did not use a gun or weapon to obtain the victim's money nor did the scammer unlawfully take the victims' belongings without their knowledge. If these were the cases, it would have been robbery or theft. Scam victims willingly gave the scammers the money, based on whatever business they had. A victim who has lost a lot of money in a scam business cannot explain in details how he or she lost the money. It is normally during this explanation that the victim realizes how stupid he or she has been. This self realization without any assistance is very common.

The scam business is complex. A good number of victims cannot even stand the shame of explaining in details how they lost money to a scammer. Many scam victims will commit business suicide if they explain how they got scammed. It is clear in most successful scams, that some of the payments such scam victims made to the scammers, were born out of sheer greed, flimsy gullible reasons, criminal intent, etc. The majority of victims just let the business go and forget about it, rather than explain the whole episode to the authorities in details. Even in cases where the scam victim reported to the authorities, he or she will try to omit certain embarrassing explanations that might jeopardize his or her integrity, thereby making the case difficult for the authorities to solve.

The best is do not get scammed because the majority of scams are very difficult to prove and you might get scammed further trying to achieve guilt on the scammer. It is common for scam victims to fear the possibility that the police and the authorities will start looking at them suspiciously; as crooked in their ways as soon as they explain the whole detailed transaction in a scam as a victim.

We have discussed earlier that scam proposals have undertones of irregularities that receivers cannot deny. Scam businesses are crooked businesses; they are uncommon businesses, improper businesses and irregular businesses, too. One participating in them will somehow be seen as crooked, too. There are very few legitimate explanations that will exonerate any participant from being guilty of greed. No matter how you got involved in a scam business, the offer (the greedy gain) was presented and you accepted it. You will need to pray that the authorities assisting you have not judged and found you guilty of greed or you might lose more money. Another reason is, to have been scammed means you are gullible to an extent. You easily believe and trust people;

In major scams like most money transfer scams, the scam victims volunteered to keep custody of some 'illegal' monies. Either monies that did not belong to them or they were claiming a payment that was not rightfully theirs.

In cases of scams that first started as normal, genuine businesses, the victims cannot say that they did not notice some atoms of illegality when the so called initial genuine business metamorphosed into another business (the ensued scam). Those signals of an illegal business clearly manifested but the victim over looked it as minor, inconsequential or boldly went ahead for the profit. Atoms of illegality are in all scams and they are normally overlooked by many scam victims only to hurt them later in the law.

Mr. John Tang, a Chinese major exporter was discussing a large order with some supposed businessmen in Nairobi. After submitting his normal quote, his business partners requested that Mr. Tang inflate the quote by 65%. They told Mr. Tang that the inflated excess will be shared 50-50 amongst them after the normal quote was paid to him. The Nairobi business partners also claimed that they had the possible government contacts and connections to get the new 65% inflated quote approved. This Mr. Tang did. They later told Mr. Tang that the new inflated quotation has been approved, and Mr. Tang submitted his account particulars for the initial 80% mobilization

**payment. After two weeks of nothing happening, Mr. Tang decided
to call them. His Nairobi business partners now informed him that
the concerned government ministry was insisting on full registration
of his company in Kenya according to the indigenous incorporation
act before such a huge supply could be awarded to a non indigenous
firm as standing Kenyan supply regulations demanded. Finally,
the whole explanations and suggestions force Mr. Tang to send
$10,000 to his business partners in Nairobi to execute the company
registration. Mr. Tang's business partners were actually scammers
from day one. Mr. Tang never got the supply nor was his company
registered, he lost his $10,000.**

This is a mixture of legalities and illegalities as is in many scams; a
genuine business is started, which metamorphosed into a bigger business
with illegal undertones and business expenses which were payments to
the scammer.

Mr. Tang cannot say that he was still doing a 100% genuine business
when he accepted to inflate his initial quote by 65%. To accept to do
the inflation shows that the original, genuine business has started
metamorphosing on minor illegalities. Mr. Tang might even claim that
his quote whether inflated or not was fully legal. He might be correct
but it was at that stage that the scam process penetrated the genuine
business. It was at that stage that Mr. Tang's required greed and targeted
commitment hatched for the eventual scam. It is also possible that Mr.
Tang, after being scammed out of the $10,000 might report to the
police authorities and will purposely omit to mention that he inflated his
original quotation by 65%. He might believe that mentioning the 65%
inflation to the police might make the police think twice about him, so
he will omit that part of the details and insist that the Nairobi partners
just duped him out of $10,000 company registration money. Mr. Tang's
case will become weaker as the police will keep wondering how on earth
he just sent $10,000 to some people he did not know very well. The
Nairobi scammers, on the other hand, might claim that he gave them
the $10,000 to help facilitate his quotation which eventually did not get
approval as other similar suppliers like Mr. Tang quoted far less.

All scam victims must do more than average to find the scammer
guilty, the business confidentiality, secrecy, greed, the varied
commitments etc, all play to the advantage of the scammer as a matter
of fact. It is common for most onlookers not to believe the scam victims;

that it was those flimsy simple reasons they are giving that made them lose so much money. Onlooker will believe that the whole story has not actually been told. A smart scammer can equally complicate the facts of the case with his or her own tallying lies.

Do not fall for a scam because it might be difficult to catch the scammer. The surest way to catch a scammer is physically in the scamming act. Catch a scammer in the physical act of impersonation and you might have the best case. Telephone records, mobile phones, websites, faxes, pictures, documents, emails, addresses, etc., can all be manufactured and deleted by choice. The scammer can deny having any of them unless caught with one. The victim's prosecution might even not be able to associate these communication mediums with the scammer. The world is now a global village and most things are now possible communication wise.

After losing close to $3,000,000 to scammers, Mr. Lewinski contacted the metropolitan police in London. Together he arranged with the police detectives to lure the scammers into a police trap in the Midcastil hotel in London. The police wanted to catch the scammers in the act with enough prosecuting proof which was the only way, since Mr. Lewinski did not have enough evidence for an earlier prosecution even if they had been arrested. The plan was set. Mr. Lewinski told the scammers that he was now willing to pay the $600,000 and endorse the final contract award papers. He insisted that the attorneys (scammers) must bring the document to his hotel room at the Midcastil hotel for him to endorse and that he would hand over the money there. The police plan was perfect but unfortunately for Mr. Lewinski, the scammers lived in London and knew their whereabouts. Under the impression that the attorneys are arriving in two days time, they quickly rented a room next to Mr. Lewinski's room in the same hotel and planted one of their colleagues there. The scammers bought two similar briefcases and dropped one in their watch room next to Mr. Lewinski's room. Finally, they called to tell Mr. Lewinski that they were coming for the meeting and believed he had the agreed $600,000. The scammers with all boldness entered the hotel to see Mr. Lewinski. The police detectives were well positioned all over the hotel premises and waited patiently. When the scammers entered Mr. Lewinski's room, Mr. Lewinski greeted them and they sat down. They excused themselves to use the

convenience after which business started. They simply brought out the documents for Mr. Lewinski to endorse which he did and gave them the $600,000. The scammers checked the money, thanked him and left. The two scammers were arrested by metropolitan police detectives in the lobby downstairs as they were leaving the hotel with their briefcase. They were taken to the metropolitan police station for further investigations. At the station, the police discovered that the said briefcase they had was empty and only contained magazines. It was outrageous as all efforts to locate the $600,000 and the incriminating documents that should have been in the briefcase were fruitless. The police held the two scammers for some hours and let them go. There was nothing to charge them with. The $600,000 was gone, vanished into thin air. Mr. Lewinski sued the police, and so on.

The scammers switched their original briefcase that had the money and endorsed documents for an empty one that contained only magazines as they left Mr. Lewinski's room. That was why they planted their colleague in the next room. Also, they must have arrived at the hotel with an empty briefcase which they switched for the one with the documents as they entered Mr. Lewinski's room. While they were arrested, their colleague in the next room simply checked out of the room in a normal fashion, and went home with the loot.

Scammers can be very bold. The lesson to learn here is that the police also know that without good evidence the scammer will walk. The scammers being criminals already know that without good evidence they will walk. Mr. Lewinski's scammers claimed at the police that Mr. Lewinski wanted them to help design a new magazine for him, so he invited them to his hotel room for final discussions. Also bear in mind that the scammer can hire good lawyers too. Many criminal defense lawyers enjoy these types of cases as long as the defender is rich. Scams are difficult to prosecute without good evidence. They are unlike theft which some people confuse as scams. Taking someone's belonging by duress or force is different. Scam is unlike buying and selling of goods where you are accountable. Many scams are not selling and buying with official receipts, unless the scammers designed the scam schemes in such ways, and that can be successfully prosecuted.

Scam businesses can be very risky and dangerous to the victims. There are cases when victims are lured into territories and robbed. These are different from scams where the victim willingly and happily parted with his or her money for the scammer. A scam proposal can have many meanings; to scam you, to steal your private information or to lure you into the scammer's comfortable territory to rob you or even blackmail you. The world we live in these days has changed so much that certain businesses might mean murder for the victim. The scammer can kill you for your money; many presumed scammers will not have that time to set a scheming plan to scam you but simply rob you, this is becoming rampant worldwide. Many scammers will kill you when you refuse to comply with directives as long as you are in their physical presence. There have been cases where foreign business persons are kidnapped and their families pay ransoms for their release. Anything is possible as long as you are a scam victim. It all lies in the hands of the scammer (your unknown business partner). Your unknown business transaction partner is very complex as a matter of fact so you must try to be able to deduce some of his or her intentions from the ongoing business processes. For instance, being able to analyze to a great extent the real purpose of an invitation letter from an unknown business partner is a great advantage.

In very successful scams with business processes, what the scam victims were paying for is difficult to define. Actually, the victims were paying for something that should materialize, which had no time limit. The materialization could be now, in the near future or in the distant future. The only available time limit is how far the victim is willing to wait for the materialization of the promised gain (or rather the victim realizes the whole business is a scam). There have been cases where the scammers still claimed in court that the business in question is still in the process of materializing, which can complicate the case further.

Judges in courts are humans too. There are cases where the scammers are found guilty not based on available evidence. It is not that presented evidence during trial was enough to convict the scammer but the judge having read in-between the lines from all cross examinations, clearly understand what must have transpired that led to the whole scam. Most societies and authorities now adopt this method to serve as a deterrent and discourager for scammers. I mention this here because very experienced scammers in an unbiased court of competent jurisdiction will sail through. To find such scammers guilty will require serious efforts. No two scams are exactly the same, so the judge would have difficulty setting a precedent. Scams are hardly defined, and majority of the victims' commitment in scams were self imposed. One therefore should not subject his or her case to the judge's ability to read in-between the lines.

Justice is three headed; justice to the accused, justice to the victim and justice in the society's perspective.

Justice can wear any of these heads that faithful day in court and you never know what will happen. Therefore, business transactions must be scrutinized thoroughly before making expenses as business costs or investments in doing business.

A clear example was the guilty verdict on a scam where some South American bank directors were scammed heavily running into hundreds of millions of dollars. Those accused persons were found guilty in order to protect the integrity of their country of origin, exonerate government involvement and to encourage further foreign investments in that country. It would have been practically discouraging for foreign investors coming to that very country if those accused persons were found not guilty.

There have been several claims that some governments are involved in some scams. I do not think that any legitimate government will purposely be involved in scams. The complications here are that some people forget to understand that the way one government functions might not be the way another government works. The best genuine advice has been made clear; do not pay scammers. When you do, make sure you positively identify the person you paid so that the government can help you.

It is improper to start asking people to help you locate your missing wrist watch in an ocean, after several warnings to remove your watch before entering the ocean.

Moreover, do not be deceived, there is minor involvement of some authorities and not necessarily government in some scams. The colonial slave trade could not have worked so well and for so long without the gainful involvement of then authorities, in those African communities were these slaves were taken from. Those authorities, then, did not fully grasp what those slaves were being used for. If they knew, maybe they would have asked for more in payment for those slaves. The American and European slave buyers then must have been telling them a different story altogether.

As earlier said, scams are legally complicated; police authorities cannot understand how a victim just wired $1,000,000, or even $10,000 to someone he or she has never know before except for some paper works or online application forms. Believe me, the scam victim just has to tell this whole story again and explain it better because it is unbelievable.

There are standing rules and laws that act as restrictions on certain financial activities to prevent scams, but these restrictions are being violated on a daily basis worldwide. Scammers still collect funds from reputable banks without proper identification papers. Scammers still secure travel visas from very strict embassies without even attending visa interviews. Telephone companies still allocate telephone lines without proper authentication of the user's identity. So many of the things you think are not possible in your place are so possible in the other man's place. Also, we must not underestimate the power an extra income has on practically everyone, even on a presumed angel. The majority of people only differ in their service price. Offer the right price and you will be surprised.

In avoiding scams, it is also important to note that payments made by a scam victim pass through so many hands, making it very difficult to recover all back, even if need be.

Do you know how many persons and businesses will benefit from a US$1,000,000 scam victims payment, which enters a remote community district?

Such a scam victim's payment to one scammer might not be all his or hers, but believe me that so many other persons and businesses will benefit. Banks will take commission; governments will take their taxes and so on. The $1,000,000 payment will increase the money supply for that community, benefiting so many persons and businesses.

Repeatedly, Western Union, Moneygram and other money transfer firms have been accused of assisting scammers. We should all understand that these are profit oriented companies who must do their businesses and only help were they can. 'Do not pay scammers' is the last wisdom. These money transfer firms have done all possible things to discourage scam victims from paying scammers but societies are vast, vary and differ. What is not possible in one place is possible in another place. It is your duty to know the scammer and not send money to him or her. The money transfer firm did not provide the name of the scammer the victim sent money to nor did the money transfer firm direct the victim on the amount to send to the scammer. The scam victim knows very well how and where he or she got information and data from, before visiting the money transfer firm to complete the transfer process. This is the simplest truth, no matter how strange.

Scams are therefore a classic mixture of legalities and illegalities. Whether the legality outweighs the illegality or vice versa, all depends on the scammer's design to affect the victim's reasoning and the victim's perception of legality.

A criminally minded would-be scam victim will still be comfortable if the ongoing business illegalities outweigh the legalities, but the self acclaimed righteous would-be scam victim will prefer more legalities than illegalities in the ongoing business transaction.

The undisputed fact is that, even an atom of illegality in an unknown business transaction is enough to make the whole unknown business transaction illegal.

PART 5

AVOIDING SCAMS

Scammers are very sophisticated and they can target people of all backgrounds, ages and income. There are no exceptions as long as the prospective victim is willing to go ahead with the scammer's proposal. There is no one group of people who are more likely to become a victim of a scam. A well developed self defense mechanism can be comfortably used to avoid scams and scammers alike.

CHAPTER 29

TRANSACTION VIGILANCE

Scammers, since time immemorial have taken advantage of any minor lapse in your vigilance. It is common in most people to find rooted lapses in their judgment of situations. Teaching old dog new tricks can be difficult but it can still be done. One of the first steps in avoiding scams is to condition your assumptions and myths so that they do not lead you into scams. To avoid scams you must not have assumptions or myths that are wrong and dangerous.

Some of these dangerous myths originate from people's backgrounds. Many people find it hard to believe that certain business stages can be imitated, that official and government documents can be accurately forged, because where they come from, it is impossible to forge such documents or they have never seen a forgery of anything before.

Below are assumptions to carefully note and be vigilant about. The vigilance should emanate from the instinct of anyone wishing to avoid scams in business transactions. Self defense is always the best defense in anything as complex as scams.

Generally adopt the attitude;
- That many scams are the first of their kind. New scams are coming up daily.
- That anyone can be a scam victim.
- That scam business can be started and concluded in the same day.
- That being scammed is not necessarily about your gullibility, the scammer's manipulation skills must also be considered.
- That not everything that appears to meet your needs and desires are genuine.
- That not all scams are after your money, your private details are equally important to a scammer.
- That you should beware of business proposals that push your buttons for a desired response.

- That delay spoil scams and scams spoil with delay. Take your time on any business venture.
- That you should never send money or give private details to people you don't know and trust.
- That you must always verify all money requests before sending money or providing private details.
- That seeking a second opinion from a family member, professional or friend is worthwhile.
- Always get independent advice if you are unsure whether an offer or request is genuine, irrespective of any confidentiality clause.
- That you should not commit yourself early in any business.
- That allowing illegality in your business transaction is true commitment.
- That you should understand as much as possible about how any business works and what your obligations are as clearly as possible.
- That you should learn as much as possible about your business partner or the business venture.
- That abusing a scammer only indicates your willingness to talk further.
- That any response to a scam proposal is a confirmation of your contact details.
- That those peoples with privileged wealth guard their secrets jealously.
- That there are no short-cuts to wealth, even if there were; they are not distributed.
- That you must protect yourself from the sentiment of reciprocating earlier favors to unknown persons.
- That you are not obliged to return financial favors to unknown persons.
- That you must beware of offers that pressure you to take up the offer immediately or you'll miss the opportunity.
- That you must beware of business schemes that must remain confidential in order to succeed.
- That you never shy away from asking for proof from your business partner in any business venture.

- That you never allow the mention or inclusion of known authorities of any field to misdirect vetting of any business proposal.
- That everybody does it does not mean it is right.
- That majority can be wrong too.
- That you never make your decisions based on what other people have agreed to.
- That nothing is the best of them until proven so.
- That no offer is the last of its kind if they are genuine.
- That coincidences do happen—you visited the bank yesterday does not mean the bank caller today is genuine, you visited London last week does not mean that the caller is someone you met in London—until proven otherwise.

While dealing with firms or companies;
- Always do your homework on any individual or company worker to ensure that they are legitimate for all business ventures.
- Legitimate companies don't pressure people to act without time to look into the deal.
- Many businesses, companies and organizations are set up from day one for scamming people.
- Not all businesses, companies and organizations are fully registered with their governments.
- Not all registered businesses, companies and organizations carry out genuine businesses.
- Not all businesses, companies and organizations registered with their governments have been vetted and approved by their government authorities.
- Any company should be able to explain to you in 30 seconds or less how they make their money. Do not let anyone brush off your questions or tell you their business is too complicated to explain.

In foreign business ventures;
- Be cautious when dealing with individuals/companies from outside your own country.
- Always remember that monies sent overseas are difficult to get back.

- Always analyze what method of payment any seller is asking and where he/she is asking to send payment.
- Do not believe the promise of large sums of money for your cooperation in a foreign business ventures.
- Always bear in mind that apart from verification difficulties in foreign businesses, prosecution can be cumbersome.
- In any business, make sure there are no unexpected costs; be very sure of every step including shipping and handling charges if not explicitly explained.
- Be skeptical of individuals representing themselves as foreign government officials asking for your help in placing large sums of money in overseas bank accounts.

While dealing with documents;
- Most documents can be forged; likewise currencies have forgeries in circulation.
- Beware of anyone with convincing documents to explain why you need to give them money or your personal details.
- Samples of most important documents can be found on the internet.

While making purchases;
- Always purchase merchandise from a reputable source.
- Never be shy to inquire about returns and warranties in any business transaction.

While investing;
- Beware of businesses and investment schemes that promise very high returns with little costs and risks.
- All investments have some degree of risk.
- All legitimate investments must have documents that explain the investment in details.
- Beware of investments with penalties for early investment termination.
- Beware of unsolicited offers described as 'tax-free wealth'.
- Don't invest in anything you are not absolutely sure of, and is government backed.

- Do your homework on the investment and the company to ensure that they are legitimate.

While online or surfing the web;
- Not all internet websites are legitimate.
- Websites can be easily set up and never difficult.
- There are paid professionals who can set up any website similar to another for a fee.
- Log directly onto websites you are interested in, rather than clicking on links provided in an email.
- Check out other websites regarding any company. Comparison helps.
- Don't judge a person or company by their website. Flashy websites can be set up quickly.
- Don't trust a site just because it claims to be secure.
- Always watch what you buy on the internet and always seek a prescription before buying medicine or healthcare.
- Never be 100% sure of who you are dealing with on the internet.
- Before using any site, always check out the security/encryption software it uses.

While answering or making calls;
- Give out little or no information on the phone.
- Be watchful of offers from callers, persons or companies who give few or no details about themselves.
- Beware of callers pushing you to provide personal information.
- Beware of callers who discourage you from checking if any request is genuine.
- Beware of callers offering to assist you repair bad credit rating.
- Always check the provided name and contact number of person calling from your bank before taking any requested action.
- Never assume to be a winner of a lottery or competition you are not sure that you entered.
- Beware of persons making educated guesses based on readily available public information such as your name and phone number they got from online directories.

- Beware, if the caller claims that your business has ordered or authorized something you do not think sounds right.

While reading or writing emails;
- Never send your credit card or bank details in an email.
- Always contact your bank with any suspicious email.
- Give out little information in writing emails.
- Beware of offers that pressure you to take up the offer immediately or you'll miss the opportunity.
- Do not rely only on an e-mail address. If it is a business, check the business affairs commission for proper verifications.
- Beware of 'private offers' emails open only to a selected few.
- Never rely on a number provided in an email or click on the provided link.
- Legitimate bank and financial institution will never email you asking you to follow a link or asking you for private details.
- Do not call your bank or financial institutions using any telephone number listed in an email, always use a number that appears on your statement or ATM card or in the telephone book.
- Be sure to send an e-mail to make sure the e-mail address is active, and be wary of those that utilize free e-mail services where a credit card wasn't required to open the email account.
- Be cautious when responding to special investment offers, especially through unsolicited e-mail.
- Beware of persons who use spam email or ads posted in the street to employ people.
- Beware of an email, SMS or a phone call out of the blue asking you to 'validate' or 'confirm' private banking details.

In meeting persons bear in mind that;
- Scammers and con men are human beings, like anyone.
- Scammers can also have attractive characteristics and irresistible personalities.
- The very rich can also scheme well-financed and sophisticated bigger scams.
- Be watchful of offers from persons who give few or no details about themselves.

- Beware of offers that pressure you to take up the offer immediately or you'll miss the opportunity.

In any business venture;
- Never shy away from asking for proof in any business venture.
- Ensure that goods have actually been ordered and delivered before paying an invoice.
- Beware of payment renewal requests and always check for the actual expiry date of all your subscriptions.
- Beware of fax backs requests and check it out properly.
- Be suspicious if you are overpaid for products.
- Be suspicious if a number of credit card numbers are used.
- Be wary of complicated or unlikely orders.
- Do not trust all publication databases.
- Some publications in some company database are free and are automatic when a trademark is registered.
- Be careful and never overlook missing amounts from your bank account without any explanations no matter the amount.

In using your cards and bank accounts;
- Always keep your personal information very safe.
- The best bank contact information is always on the back of your ATM card.
- Make sure the transaction is secure when you electronically send your credit card numbers.
- Shred all documents containing personal information, such as credit card applications and bank statements.
- If possible, purchase items online using your credit card, because you can often dispute the charges if something goes wrong.
- Regularly check your credit card and/or bank statements to ensure that suspicious transactions are detected.
- Consider using an escrow or alternate payment service.
- Don't give out your credit card number online unless the site is secure and reputable. Sometimes a tiny icon of a padlock appears to symbolize a higher level of security to transmit data. This icon is not a guarantee of a secure site, but provides some assurance.
- Keep a list of all your credit cards and account information along with the card issuer's contact information. If anything looks

suspicious or you lose your credit card(s), contact the card issuer immediately.
- Be careful and never overlook missing amounts from your bank account without any explanations no matter the amount.
- Beware for identity theft is real and a long way to come out of.

Avoiding scams may be hard, especially for first-timers and new business persons coming across scams for the first time, but, there are ways to be safe from them. Apart from being on the lookout for the compulsory scam business process features mentioned in this book, one wishing to avoid a scam can take simple precautions such as;

Monitoring your credit. The very first step in any financial freedom quest is to be able to know exactly what happens to your money. What is the fate of the very money in your pocket as you read this now? It is priority in all financial endeavors to have a good knowledge of what happens to your income—before and after you earned it. If you cannot deduce exactly where your income is going, no matter how small it is, then you have a serious problem, which must be solved immediately.

One can also be cautious **by *making payments with a cheque instead of cash*;** Checks are the safest way to pay for most things. A cheque passes through many channels that will give the issuer enough advantage to verify anything suspicious before final payment is made to the cheque beneficiary. The issuer must be quite knowledgeable of what to check for as his or her cheque passes bank clearing. Scammers and deceivers oftentimes transact with cash as they can easily get away with it. Checks require a process, and scammers do not like it; they have to create fake identity cards, papers, etc., which will definitely risk their exposure to the law. Also, do not make the mistake of wiring money often. Internet banking has made it possible for one to be in New York and be retrieving funds in a Melbourne bank on a daily basis. There is no guarantee that you could get your deposit back if you wired it to a fake person in Germany, who will withdraw the wired funds from a totally different bank in South Africa and not even in Germany, where the original account was domiciled. You cannot track anyone; most banks do not like such expenses and are busy with 'more careful' customers.

Everyone in a business transaction must ***do one's homework.*** This is compulsory and if you cannot do your homework then the business is not worth for you to even consider. I believe that people who cannot do their homework are busy people. They should keep up with whatever they are doing and leave new businesses aside. Verify all and crosscheck all. Never be in a hurry and ask questions from professionals where applicable. Businesses have always existed and there is no new business secret that the world could not hear now. Do your homework as part of business costs. No free lunch.

Detecting fake websites is another precaution to take while on the internet. In doing this, fraud cues as well as problems-specific knowledge are important. Fraud cues are the information, navigation and visual design that indicate a website is not authentic while the problem-specific knowledge discloses the unique properties of fake websites, which includes stylistic similarities and content duplications.

Meet physically where necessary. It is always better to meet your business partners physically. Select safe locations for a business meeting. Physical assessment has saved many prospective victims from being scammed. Inasmuch as some scammers can also arrange all these physical meetings, it can never be perfect if the suspecting party has prepared very well for the meeting with adequate questions to ask. Genuine persons prefer physical meetings and are never in a hurry to make any payment. Remember that scammers are only out to get your money, and the quickest possible way is always the best for them. Never see hurry as time saving for you.

Make ***no advance payments,*** no matter what is at stake. Any business that requires an advance payment has created enough room for suspicion. There are letters of credit, bank guarantees and post-dated checks which are legal tenders and commitments that stand in court, so why make quick advance payments to anyone if you believed you were doing something genuine.

A CONCLUSION

People victimized by scammers vary every year, but is always on the increase. Every successful scam encourages other scammers still searching for their ideal scam victims. Scams propagate and even evolve each time better than the last. Avoiding scams and working hard for your daily bread should be treated equally; both are very important in life. It would be sad to work so hard, for, at the very end, lose all the hard work to a simple scam that could have been prevented. The current economic crunch has not only brought financial woes for most people but also an outpouring of swindlers and scammers on the prowl for some prospective scam victims.

Scams and scammers are no longer strange to anyone; they are so common that I am sure almost everyone actively working for a living must have come across one scam scheme or the other. Such situations will continue as long as new advancements in communication, technology and the internet are being made; the scam schemes and scam proposals one comes across will become more frequent.

Imagine the work done by the good party to develop spam box in filtering your unwanted emails from your email inbox and also think of the work done by the other party in developing software that will deliver unwanted emails directly to inboxes. This has become the sequence of almost everything in our world today. One party works hard for 'good', the other party works hard for 'bad'. It is worth acknowledging and understanding that both are in business to make money.

Generally when the economy flattens, scammers are known to come up with innovative ways to scam people out of their money. Likewise, in uncertain financial times, consumers are more willing to take desperate risks to relieve the burdens of unemployment, foreclosure, and debt.

It is very important to understand that;
'A good lie is based in truth'.

Scammers' heaven has been created with the recession; most people have financial problems and are looking for a way out of these financial problems. Since the general recession began, financial scams have increased, Scammers look for things on the news that will help them connect with their unsuspecting victims. They have learned that a good lie is based in truth, which is why some scams schemes are especially confusing.

We must understand that so many people believe in the news or directives from our governments, that scammers now use these news stories to their advantage, setting up websites that imitate those of official government agencies, or tax units. They even act like couriers pretending to deliver your parcel when their main mission is to steal your signature or steal your identity. Scammers exploit timely topics like identity fraud protection efforts by banks. Scammers invading Europe and America due to the recession, now use topics such as bank closings, tax breaks, and government giveaways related to the government's economic stimulus plan to incite interest from prospective scam victims. These kinds of scammers are known as pretexters (because they contact you under a false pretext). They call or e-mail consumers and urge them to fill out forms on these sites in order to receive bogus tax refunds, recover money lost in a bank closing, or recoup investments stolen from them in a scam.

The recession has brought so much unemployment, of which scammers are also taking advantage. Employment scams are on the rise. Scammers showcase enticing job offers and job advertisements have become a way to cheat job seekers out of their money. Scammer's are using employment interviews to lure their victims into their desired scam stages.

In the United States, The housing foreclosure crisis is yet another high-profile news story that scammers use to prey on consumers. In some instances, con artists tell a homeowner they can prevent the home from going into foreclosure for a fee. Scammers have promised to pay the mortgage for homeowners who sign over their deeds and pay rent. In both instances, owners are advised not to contact their lenders because any interference could jeopardize the new mortgage terms. The homeowner in these scams simply loses the house and no longer owns the deed, yet remains responsible for the mortgage. Such scam victims take the credit hit while the scammer gets away with the fee and, in some cases, rent money.

Another precaution worth taking while on the internet is to have and assign different email addresses for different purposes. It will enable a better understanding of the emails you receive. When I separated my website interacting email address from my personal email address, I discovered a significant decrease in the junk emails and scam proposals I receive in my personal email address.

Now that you have finished reading this book, you have confirmed your knowledge in avoiding scams or you are now better equipped to avoid scams. Either way, your confidence in handling your next business transaction and what to look out for, has increased. One obstacle globalization must overcome is scam. Thank you.

BIBLIOGRAPGHY

Bearing in mind that the best searches for information on avoiding scams are in the internet, many authors have also mentioned or touched on materials that somehow relate to some topics mentioned in this book where I have elaborated on my personal opinion on how best preventing being scammed.

Below are some of these literatures and their authors; likewise are very useful websites with information that will aid anyone in avoiding scams. These literatures and websites assisted me in developing my concepts on some topics mentioned in this book and also aided in my understanding of what I presume, actually happens in scam situations.

I will not fail to thank some renowned authors whose works made me believe to start putting this book together. I have already mentioned most of them below but there are two authors whose works were exceptional to me in the articulation and writing of the **Unknown Transactions**.

First is Robert Greene's '*The 48 Laws of Power*' and Herb Cohen's works, '*You Can Negotiate Anything*' and '*Negotiate This*'. These three works have had a great impact on my understanding of possible relationships that can exist in peculiar situations of negotiations.

Other recommended literatures are;
Alexrod, R. *The Evolution of Cooperation.* Basic Books (1984)
Blau, P. *Exchange and Power in Social life.* Wiley (1964)
Cialdini R. B. *Influence: The Psychology of Persuasion.* Harper Business (2006)
Cohen, H. *Negotiate This.* Warner Books (2003)
Cohen, H. *You Can Negotiate Anything.* Bantam (1980)
Gottschalk, P. *Policing Cyber Crime.* Petter Gottschalk & Ventus Publishing ApS (2010)
Greene, R. *The 48 Laws of Power.* Profile Books (2000)
Hewward-Mills, D. *Loyalty and Disloyalty.* Parchment House (2005)
Heider, F. *The Psychology of Interpersonal Relations.* Wiley (1958)
Jeffrey G. R. *Finding Financial Freedom.* Water Brook Press (2005)
Krause D. G., *The Art of War for Executives.* Nicholas Brealey Books (1995)
Machiavelli, N. *The Prince.* Pengium Books: George Bull Translation (1999)
Odulaja, K. *No Dreams No Destiny.* Prevailing Word Publications (2003)

Tenney, T. *The God Chasers.* Destiny Image (1998)

Trudeau, K. *Free Money: They Don't Want You to Know About.* Equity Press (2009)

Trump, D. and M Schwartz. *The Art of the Deal.* Random House (1992)

Wizard B. *Nigerian 419 Scam 'Game Over'* Starquill International (2000)

Wizard B. *'Don't Be Scammed—Be Informed'* Starquill international (2006)

Zagorin, P. *Ways of Lying: Dissimulation, Persecution and Conformity in Early Modern Europe.* Cambridge: Harvard University Press, (1990)

Zartman, W. *The Negotiation Process.* Sage (1978)

Helpful websites in avoiding scams;

http://419.bittenus.com/photos.htm

http://money.howstuffworks.com/personal-finance/financial-planning/investment-scams.htm

http://opinion.inquirer.net/45671/guarding-against-investment-scams

http://www.acma.gov.au/WEB/STANDARD/pc=PC_310047

http://www.ageuk.org.uk/money-matters/consumer-advice/scams-advice/

http://www.autotrader.com/fraud/index_pop.jsp

http://www.bankrate.com/brm/news/investing/20020829a.asp

http://www.brianwizard.com

http://www.casaswap.com/avoid-scam-on-the-internet

http://www.consumer.ftc.gov/articles/0060-10-ways-avoid-fraud

http://www.craigslist.org/about/scams

http://www.crimes-of-persuation.com

http://www.crimes-of-persuasion.com/Crimes/Business/nigerian.htm

http://www.dfsa.ae/Pages/Alerts/HowToAvoidBeingScammed.aspx

http://www.419eater.com/

http://www.fairtrading.nsw.gov.au/Consumers/Scams/Avoiding_scams.html

http://www.fairtrading.qld.gov.au/scams-and-fraud.htm

http://www.fbi.gov/scams-safety/fraud

http://www.forexoma.com/the-scams-that-you-have-to-know-and-avoid-2/

http://www.fraud.org/

http://www.fraudlabspro.com/?gclid=CNWZg8LogbYCFcHHtAodzCIAKQ

http://www.fraudwatchers.org/forums/showthread.php?t=27280

http://www.fsa.gov.uk/scams

http://www.investopedia.com/university/scams/scams1.asp#axzz2NnXNTFWi
http://www.ipaidabribe.com/?utm_source=google&utm_medium=adwords&utm_campaign=a-corruption
http://www.loanscamalert.org/
http://www.microsoft.com/security/online-privacy/phishing-scams.aspx
http://www.nigeriamasterweb.com/419NewsFrmes.html
http://www.onguardonline.gov/articles/0001-avoiding-online-scams
http://www.rd.com/advice/saving-money/7-online-scams-and-how-to-avoid-them/
http://www.ripandscam.com
http://www.scambusters.org/
http://www.scam.com/showthread.php?t=142006
http://www.scamwatch.gov.au
http://www.scamwebsites.co.uk/
http://www.scamwebsites.co.uk/avoid-these-scam-websites.html
http://www.staysmartonline.gov.au/home_users/protect_yourself2/avoiding_scams_and_hoaxes
http://www.stop-scammers.com/
http://www.usa.gov/Citizen/Topics/Internet-Fraud.shtml
http://www.us-cert.gov/sites/default/files/publications/emailscams_0905.pdf

About The Author

Kelechi Ononuju is a Biochemistry graduate, investigative reporter and development researcher. His experiences as a business executive span over a broad range of issues which include business, politics and society, to mention a few. His analytical approach to investigations, provide the needed details of 'how' and 'why' of a prominent issue.

Unknown Transactions: *avoiding scams through understanding* is his first book, apart from his papers presented at seminars and workshops. His new book, "*Trailing the Corruption: a perspective*" will be out soon. Kelechi lives in Nigeria.